Conversations with (and about) Beckett

Mel Gussow has written *Conversations with Pinter* and *Conversations with Stoppard*, two previous volumes in this series. As a longtime drama critic for the New York Times, he was a winner of the George Jean Nathan Award for Dramatic Criticism.

He has written Profiles for the New Yorker (on Athol Fugard, Bill Irwin, Peggy Ramsay and Michael Gambon) and for the New York Times Magazine. He is also the author of *Don't Say Yes Until I Finish Talking: a Biography of Darryl F. Zanuck.*

He was the recipient of a Guggenheim Fellowship and for three years served as the president of the New York Drama Critics Circle. Before joining the Times, he was a critic and cultural writer for Newsweek Magazine. A graduate of Middlebury College, he holds a master's degree in journalism from Columbia University.

by the same author

Conversations with Pinter
Conversations with Stoppard

Mel Gussow

Conversations with (and about) Beckett

Nick Hern Books
London

For Ann and Ethan

A Nick Hern Book

Conversations with (and about) Beckett first published
in Great Britain in 1996 by Nick Hern Books Ltd,
14 Larden Road, London W3 7ST

Copyright © 1996 Mel Gussow

A CIP catalogue record for this book is available
from the British Library

Typeset by Country Setting, Woodchurch,
Kent, TN26 3 TB, and printed in Great Britain by
Mackays of Chatham

ISBN 1-85459-310-2 (hardback)
ISBN 1-85459-315-3 (paperback)

Mel Gussow has asserted his right to be identified as
the author of this work

Contents

Introduction

In October 1948, seeking relief from the blackness of prose, Samuel Beckett began writing a play. As he had with his novels, he wrote it in French because he wanted the discipline of working in a foreign language. Four months later, he finished it and titled it *En attendant Godot*, soon to be translated (by Beckett himself) as *Waiting for Godot*. Then, as now, it was not clear who or what Godot was, or what the origin of the name was. Although Beckett had written a previous play, *Eleutheria*, *Waiting for Godot* became his first produced theatrical work. It was the most astonishing début of a playwright in our century, the play that was to alter the course of contemporary theatre.

When Beckett completed *Godot*, it was the climax of an *annus mirabilis*. In a little more than 12 months he had written, among other works, *Godot* and the first two parts of his trilogy of novels (*Molloy* and *Malone Dies*). Despite the eventual publication (in 1938) of the novel *Murphy* after it had been rejected by more than 40 publishers, he remained unknown. He found a publisher, Jérôme Lindon, for the trilogy, but the play went from producer to producer without arousing interest. It was Beckett's wife, Suzanne, who became his unofficial and tireless agent. As Beckett acknowledged in one of our conversations, submitting the play to producers was 'like giving it to the concierge'.

Finally they found Roger Blin. Faced with the choice of *Eleutheria* or *Godot*, he selected *Godot*, at least partly because it had a much smaller cast and would be far less costly to produce. From the moment of the opening of the play on 5 January 1953 at the Théâtre de Babylone, Paris, Beckett's future course was set and his anonymity was lost. He was not, however, surrounded by adulation. Outside of France, his detractors considerably outnumbered his admirers.

For unexplained reasons, Michael Myerberg opened the first United States production of *Waiting for Godot* at the Coconut Grove Playhouse in Miami (in January 1956), with Bert Lahr as its star. The audience, apparently expecting a typical Bert Lahr comedy, greeted it with stunned amazement. The production was abandoned and then revived three months later with Lahr still playing Estragon, but with Herbert Berghof replacing Alan Schneider as director and with E.G. Marshall replacing Tom Ewell as Vladimir. *Godot* opened at the John Golden Theatre on Broadway on 19 April 1956, six days after Samuel Beckett turned 50 – and its reception might have caused him to age prematurely. In contrast to their peers in Paris, most of the American critics were confused and out of tune with Beckett, though not all of them were as philistine as Marya Mannes in The Reporter magazine. After the London production, she had written, 'I doubt whether I have seen a worse play.' In the New York Times, Brooks Atkinson called the play 'a mystery wrapped in an enigma'.

In an ill-advised attempt to attract an élitist public, Myerberg advertised for '7000 intellectuals' to come to his rescue; they did not immediately appear. After 59 performances, the play closed. At the end of the season, the New York Drama Critics Circle named *Long Day's Journey into Night* as the best play and *Waltz of the Toreadors* as the best foreign play. There were votes for three other foreign plays, but not one for *Waiting for Godot*. It was not the public but the critics who were uncomprehending; theatregoers scarcely had a chance to register an opinion. What disturbed critics, as much as anything, was the play's apparent lack of movement. Beckett's approach was so radical that it provoked fierce resistance. Overlooked were the eloquence of the language and the author's view of life as a cosmic vaudeville.

Tantalised by the controversy, I simply showed my Columbia University I.D. at the box office and was admitted free. The theatre was half full. Later it would become fashionable for people to say that Lahr distorted Beckett's vision. The fact is that he was challenged by the role and became a Beckett tramp waiting with his life's companion for a fate that never arrived, for a faith that remained unfulfilled. If Marshall's Vladimir (or Didi) seemed like a second banana, it was a natural result of the casting. Along with his hauteur, Marshall practised a kind of wry self-effacement, and Kurt Kasznar and Alvin Epstein were superb as Pozzo and Lucky. I left the theatre that day in a state close to euphoria, wondering at the strange events that had transpired on stage. In subsequent years, I saw more than a dozen different *Godot*s, including the definitive German language version, but none has replaced the freshness of that first production when one really did not know if Godot would come.

Eventually I was to see and to review all Beckett's plays, those he had written for radio and television as well as those for the stage (and also dramatisations of his prose pieces). The productions represented a broad range of directorial approach, performances that were scrupulously faithful to the original text as well as others that were freely interpretative and transported Beckett to unlikely circumstances. The plays were presented in various countries and languages, in the most intimate chamber productions, site specific environments and on large public stages. Those captured on video included Jack MacGowran's 'lost' tape of *Krapp's Last Tape*. In a few, Beckett's drama was altered to serve a director's will. Many carried actors to new heights of accomplishment.

Together with his novels, the plays form a body of work unmatched for its intensity and its cohesiveness. Through his creativity, Beckett directly confronted the nature of being, the fact that man is born 'astride the grave'. From birth to death is the narrowest stretch of mortality, which Beckett filled with art of the most redemptive kind, art to help him – and us – survive. His vision was as humane as it was tragic.

Beckett's influence on other playwrights is immeasurable. Harold Pinter, Tom Stoppard, Edward Albee, Sam Shepard, David Mamet, Fernando Arrabal, Athol Fugard and others are, in varying degrees, sons of Beckett. He redefined the nature of playwriting, freeing it from traditional bonds of length, plot, character development, specificity of atmosphere and stage movement. In his hands, stasis became a dramatic art. *Waiting for Godot* has no beginning or end; it is all middle, but with an inner logic and a progression. Didi and Gogo wait. Godot does not come. Life goes on. The play and life repeat themselves.

Rosencrantz and Guildenstern are Stoppard's Didi and Gogo, trying to decipher history on the basis of insufficient evidence. Pinter's room – a basement, a bedroom – could be compared to a Beckett enclosure, sealed and self-defining. *Tongues* by Shepard and Joseph Chaikin is a Beckettian dream of consciousness. Directors as well as writers bear the signature of Beckett even when they are staging the work of others. Taking his key from Jan Kott, Peter Brook correlated *King Lear* with *Endgame*, with a maddened monarch becoming a Beckett tramp, keeping a silent vigil over an incomprehensible world.

Time and the theatre caught up with *Godot* and with Beckett. The Broadway 'enigma' evolved into a phenomenal international success. The play is taught, debated and produced with regularity around the world, in theatres, schools, prisons, and the words Godot and Beckettian entered everyday language. Even as it became the seminal play of the experimental theatre, *Godot* had political emanations as an expression of people and nations moving from world war to cold war, waiting impatiently for resolution while hoping to avoid apocalypse. One needed only to see the black South African version with John Kani and Winston Ntshona to realise the play's universality. In that production, it became a personal South African experience, about the endless wait for emancipation, while still retaining its wider applicability. What is so provocative about the metaphor of Godot is that he (or it) can never be definitively identified. One waits because there is no reasonable alternative.

Because he was an explorer with images and emotions as well as with words, Beckett's work was thought to be difficult, although his actors, from Bert Lahr to Billie Whitelaw, intuitively knew what he was doing. As Beckett might have said to perplexed theatregoers, 'Try again, fail better.' However, even as people came to accept his major plays (*Godot*, *Endgame*) and his trilogy of novels as masterpieces, the work became even more demanding. His later plays and prose were brief and terse. Some had the appearance of abandoned works, but each was a precise encapsulation. *Not I*, *Footfalls* and *Rockaby* are paradigms of distillation: no more need be said. Late Beckett is also nurtured by his investigation of the possibilities of theatre, a theatre in which sound and movement could supersede words.

Contemplating the art of Beckett, one necessarily wonders about the source of his tragicomic view of life. Did it come to him, in a flash, as it did with Krapp in *Krapp's Last Tape*? After 'a year of profound gloom and indigence', Krapp found himself 'that memorable night in March, at the end of the jetty, in the howling wind, never to be forgotten, when suddenly I saw the whole thing . . . the dark I have always struggled to keep under is in reality my most unshatterable association.' Interestingly, this moment of personal revelation is interrupted by Krapp stopping, starting and cursing his tape. Something similar occurs during Lucky's soliloquy in *Godot*, as Didi and Gogo respond with a 'general outcry', instead of listening to Lucky's chaotic but prescient message about the collapse of civilisation. It is almost as if Beckett himself did not want to accept the full bleakness of his own vision. But he did, and he transmuted it into art.

Before Beckett and I met, I thought about writing a biography of him, and contacted him with that objective in mind. He discouraged the idea by saying that he could be of no help to a biographer. About the same time, Deirdre Bair made a similar request and received a similar response, but she plunged ahead with her book. I decided to try to get to know him, and in so doing to achieve a greater understanding of the art and the artist. Over the course of a dozen years, I visited him almost annually in Paris, and we exchanged letters, his written in his spidery longhand.

From the first, our conversations were candid and unrecorded. He allowed me to take no notes, but after every meeting I wrote down everything I could remember in my journal. This became a private record, to be saved and savoured. These conversations form the core of this book, the story of my personal and critical journey into the world of Beckett. In our meetings, we covered a wide diversity of subjects: the theatre, sports, politics, art, Paris. It was only with reluctance that he spoke about his work. This was an area that seemed to cause him discomfort, but, in response to my persistence, he would offer glimpses, talking about his method of writing and about the extreme difficulty and urgency of his creativity. He wrote, he said, because 'all else failed', and he continued to write out of a sense of obligation: it was his duty to himself.

To outsiders, Beckett was a figure of great austerity and hermetic elusiveness. Despite all appearances, he was compassionate, inquisitive and trusting, opening himself up to the needs and demands of others: actors, other playwrights, children of friends, academics studying his work, those with legitimate reasons to meet him. Although he was reported to be adamant in his objections to all variations in production, he was flexible and not one to offer casual indictments of performances he had not seen. He was in fact a vulnerable spirit, once one moved past the initial wall of self-protectiveness.

In conversations with Jack MacGowran, Billie Whitelaw and others, the accessibility and the generosity are additionally affirmed. He touched many lives, deeply. Edward Beckett makes it clear that his uncle took an almost paternal interest in him and his education. During his nephew's years in Paris, they met weekly – for dinner, a movie or a game of billiards. As might be expected, Beckett was also humorous, in person as well as in his work. Though outwardly dour, it was the comedy of life that got him through the day. He could see the absurdities all around him. Once I characterised his humour as uproarious pessimism, a description he accepted with alacrity.

He had the most striking presence of anyone I have ever met. He looked as Samuel Beckett should look: he was as tall and as craggy as a Giacometti sculpture. Irene Worth said that he looked like an eagle. One thing was certain: there are no bad photographs of Beckett. The intensity of his art was reflected in his gaze: he was always alert and observant, and he was interested in what others had to say. When he spoke, he exuded Irish lyricism; our loss is that his voice was not recorded. Beckett's last tape, if it ever existed, would be a marvellous legacy. Those of us who were fortunate enough to hear him speak and to know him will have our memories.

Through the intervention of Alan Schneider, among others, he was aware of what I had written about his plays. The year before he died, he said to me, 'I want to thank you for everything you have done for the work in America.' Recalling Gogo's use of the word, 'Crritic!', as the ultimate insult, I took that as the ultimate compliment.

MEL GUSSOW,
February 1996

Prelude

Bert Lahr, June 1966

'We tried it out in Miami, which was like trying it out in a truant school'

B ert Lahr was acting in Aristophanes' The Birds *in Ypsilanti, Michigan, playing the founder of Cloudcuckooland. Whether he was gargling Greek names ('Agamem-nem-nem') or caterwauling 'On the Road to Mandalay,' he was outrageously funny, as he had been in* Waiting for Godot. *We met for breakfast. He drank seven cups of coffee, which may account for the adrenalin that seemed to fuel his non-stop monologue. Before I could get a word in about Beckett, he began talking about his career.*

BL: I've been in every facet of the theatre, first in carnivals, Harry Six's Southwestern New England Carnival. I was in a school act. I was about 15, doing the same sort of thing as the Marx Brothers did then, or Smith and Dale. Then, Tab shows on the Spiegelberg circuit. We would steal all the Broadway shows. Small-time vaudeville. Then, burlesque. From burlesque to big-time vaudeville, big-time vaudeville to Broadway. Radio. Television. Pictures. *The Wizard of Oz.* Musical comedies. Broadway dramatic shows, like *Burlesque.* On television, I did *Androcles, School for Wives,* Saroyan, *Visit to a Small Planet, DuBarry.* Then, *Waiting for Godot.* Tynan's review is the review I'm most proud of. Do you have his book? You can look it up. [Tynan said it was 'one of the noblest performances I have ever seen.'] *Godot* was the thing I liked best, although I only had an inkling what it was about. But what I think is as good as that of the next fella.

I had a chance to do opera, but I turned it down. I thought it was Jack Pearl calling: 'This is Mr. Bing.' I said this is Mr.

Bang. O.K., Bing, Bang! I gotcha. Then he convinced me he was Rudolf Bing. I apologised profusely. He said, 'Would you like to do *The Gypsy Baron*?' He wanted me to sing in my vibrato. But I had a show with Nancy Walker. *Girls Against the Boys,* which was a flop. Opera is the only form of show business I haven't done. I did Autolycus in *The Winter's Tale.* I was named best Shakespearean actor that year, and I have a scroll to prove it.

MG: But what about *Godot*?

BL: Beckett was a disciple of Joyce. Joyce was an anti-Anglophile. If you remember Pozzo, he was a fat man. He was dressed like John Bull and he had an emaciated fellow, Lucky, with a rope around his neck. He beat him with a whip and threw chicken bones at him. Pozzo and Lucky are symbols for England and Ireland. I think Vladimir and – what the hell part did I play? – Gogo. They're one man. The animal was Gogo. All he thought about were physical things: sex, eating, turnips, sleeping. He had no regard for more esoteric things, whereas Vladimir was always looking. He was searching for the cerebral, like a parent. Both qualities are inherent in man. They couldn't get along with one another. But they're tied together.

MG: What are they waiting for?

BL: Tomorrow. Anything. Waiting, waiting, waiting, waiting. For their wives. For wealth. Everything. It's sort of a mystery play. It leads you to the point where you think Godot is God, then it twists. It isn't God, it's human. People said, it's not a play, it's just symbols. Is it metaphysical thought? It was against all basic rules of comedy. Don't make fun of a blind man. But Beckett planned Pozzo. He made him such a heavy, you didn't give a goddamn what happened to him. When we beat him, they screamed with laughter. We played games with him.

MG: What did you think when you first read the play?

BL: It fascinated me. I kept reading and reading. What the

hell is this? My wife said, 'I think you should do it. It's a departure.' I knew I could be this lost soul.

MG: How did you approach the role?

BL: I do everything by instinct rather than studiously analysing the part. I learn the thing by rote first and sort of analyse it in a way, but I don't go beneath the meaning. I feel the part. When I did Shakespeare, I didn't know about the meaning of words in the Elizabethan era. I didn't know what doxy meant. I'm not that literate. I have to have meat and potatoes. I never knew Aristophanes was a writer of comedy. I did this stuff in burlesque. His stuff is all such fun and satire – of religion, legislators, avarice, war. He was a reformer, even more than Dickens. That's what I think in my unerudite way.

I worry whether I'm going to be good in a show. I'm known as a worrier. Worry is a form of selfishness. Will Rogers said, 'A fellow who doesn't worry is either crazy or drunk.' You can look up his quote. With me, it relates back to my insecurity as a kid. I was a very lazy kid until I fell into show business. Then I was too ambitious. If the act didn't go over, I worried tremendously. Years ago, I couldn't sleep the night before a show, whereas Ethel Merman, she's Fort Sumter. This stage of life, I'm mellow. What the hell do I have to prove? I don't want to work too hard. I want to fish. I don't think there's any such thing as a good fisherman. Just stupid fish.

MG: Did you have any doubts about *Godot*?

BL: We tried it out in Miami, which was like trying it out in a truant school. The biggest flop in the history of the theatre. After the opening, there were 10 people out there. But then Tallulah Bankhead came. She was going to do *A Streetcar Named Desire*, and she said, 'You're the only one who has the right instinct for this.' I told Myerberg, 'This is a funny show, too,' so I insisted on approval of the director and of the cast if we were to come to New York. Herbert Berghof became the director. We immediately had a rapport. It was one of the most satisfying things. They didn't applaud. They just stood up.

19

Jack MacGowran, 9 January 1973

'Near the Martello Tower is a house with a woman named Mrs. Pozzo. She has a serving maid called Lucky'

After Beckett won the Nobel Prize in 1969, there was a quickening of interest in his work. In the next few years, there were two Off-Broadway productions of Waiting for Godot, *one in which Tom Ewell finally played Didi in New York, as well as productions of* Endgame *and Beckett's shorter pieces. In November 1970, Jack MacGowran presented his solo evening from the works of Beckett. The following May, I wrote to Beckett suggesting that we meet when I was in Paris that summer. Beckett responded with a note saying that he had read my review of the MacGowran show with much pleasure. He said that his plans for the summer were still uncertain and he could not commit himself to a date. Then he added unequivocally, 'I do not give interviews in any shape or form and would have to ask you to regard our meeting as a strictly private one.' As it turned out, when I was in Paris in July, he was in Santa Margherita in Italy.*

Two years later, I spoke to MacGowran when he was acting in The Plough and the Stars *at Lincoln Centre. The conversation centered on his two favourite playwrights, Beckett and Sean O'Casey. He began by talking about his drinking problem.*

JM: I've drunk enough to sink a battleship. I was a social drinker but I stopped when I became an antisocial drinker. When I found myself going from the bed to the vodka bottle, a red light went off. More drinks were consumed at Stratford. O'Toole, Patrick Wymark were there. We were all trapped.

20

There was only one professional, Michael Langham. Peter Hall and John Barton were undergraduates. Now they're professionals. They were trying to give Shakespeare meaning he never had. In the same way, people read into Beckett meaning he never had. The pub became the place to be anaesthetised. If I hadn't stopped drinking, I could never have done the Beckett anthology. I knew it would have to be a complete cut-out. It demanded a five-year study of complete concentration on everything he wrote. Preparing the anthology meant getting to know the man.

MG: What did you learn about the man?

JM: It's not true that Beckett is shy, evasive, a philosopher of the ivory tower, a philosopher of despair. He's written about human distress not human despair. Everything in his work ends with hope. Hope, hope, in everything he writes. I've never met a man with so much compassion for the human race. Joyce was the centre of attraction. He loved himself. He was the hub around which everything revolved. Beckett is the wheel that revolves around a hub.

MG: What's his hub?

JM: Humankind. I can't count the number of people he helped, financially or otherwise. He cares nothing for material things. He divested himself of material things except for the few things he likes. I think he gave his Nobel Prize money away.

MG: When did you first meet Beckett?

JM: I was doing *All That Fall*. It hit me here [he touched his stomach]. I couldn't say why. It was something for me, plumbing the depths. I knew the terrain. It had tremendous images of parts of Ireland. Then I read *Waiting for Godot* and his essay on Proust. I became more involved with his writing. I said to Donald McWhinnie, 'It's not idle curiosity but I have to meet him.' Sam came to London [in 1961]. They were doing *Endgame* at the Royal Court and he was staying at the Royal Court Hotel. When you see someone who you admire so much you don't know what to say. He was a tall athletic figure with a donnish head, a beautifully loosely-carried man.

Donald fled. I was afraid. At that time I was drinking. Beckett drank Irish whiskey and lager. There was dead silence. He looked at the floor. Every furrow on his face seemed to be in deep. He thinks I'm going to pester him. Then I became silent. I couldn't think of anything to say. I must have been utterly tight after a half hour. I cracked and suddenly blurted out something about a rugby match. He said something about a rugby match, and we talked about rugby, golf, six-day bicycle riding. Not a word about literature.

What surprised me was his Dublin accent. After enough whiskies, I said, 'I detect tones of Dublin.' 'That's right, I was born in Dublin.' About three miles from where I lived. That explains why we gelled so well. I understood his rhythm, his terrain. Later I travelled to Paris. We discussed his work. I had to try to get into his intellect to a large degree. Having found his life style, I thought this is going to be like the re-entry of astronauts into earth orbit. I tried to go into his intellect and came out very shaken. My whole philosophy of life had changed.

MG: How do you go into someone's intellect?

JM: It's like emptying your own head completely. You let your self drift into his consciousness. It's almost a mesmeric thing, without his knowing it. When I came to, I was quite shattered. The rewards were tremendous. I learned so much about human compassion. There's no use scratching the surface of Beckett. You have to go deep into him. As a result of going that far, I could do the anthology. He said, 'On paper my novels are very difficult to understand.' I went to Sam with the anthology, and whenever there were sentences that had literary quality, he cut them out.

There are many avenues of approach, ways of looking at things. The first avenue is the simple thread. It can't be that, but with Beckett it is, as it is with all great writers. He said, 'People read great symbolism I never intended.' I remember someone asking him who Godot was and he said, 'I'll tell you one thing. He's not God.' Godot is a well-known French surname, and one person who has it is a well-known racing cyclist. He did not explain his work because he thought, 'I will feel superior to my own work if I try to explain it.'

When I was having trouble with *Endgame*, I sent for Beckett. He came over and put it on a straight line. George Devine was Hamm, I was Clov. Poor George was too avuncular for Hamm. Another time, Beckett asked me to play *Endgame* in Paris. He said, 'Could I have Patrick Magee play Hamm?' I conned Patrick into playing it, against his agent's wishes, and it changed his life. Sam directed it. We played for six weeks in London, nine weeks in Paris. It was absolutely the definitive production of *Endgame*. Then we played a full season at the Aldwych.

MG: How is Beckett as a director?

JM: He's a great director. He directed my anthology in Paris. There were long pauses of 10 minutes while Beckett looked to the floor. Then he said two or three sentences, and the whole thing was clear. He is very concerned with movement, with the way a head should be turned.

MG: Did Beckett ever act?

JM: He's too shy. He would never act in a million years . . . He and Suzanne have no children. Inside the theatre, the lights come on. The theatre becomes his family, his children . . . Together we saw Olivier's *Uncle Vanya*. He didn't like it. The Irish are more in tune with Chekhov than the English are. Beckett's not been done in Russia. His philosophy was never accepted by the Soviet Union. Germany adores him; Germany pulls out every tragic note.

He wrote a play for me, *Eh Joe*. I was a lip speaker. I had to feel, not think. That's the most exhausting play of his I ever played, 20 minutes. I said, 'My gosh, Sam, you're getting more and more difficult.' *Imagination Dead Imagine* was a novel of 260 pages. I asked him, 'How's the novel?' He said, 'I've cut it down to 18 pages. That's all I could rescue from the original.' The poetic imagery is so strong. [The talk turned to Ireland.] Near the Martello Tower in Dublin is a house with a woman named Mrs. Pozzo. She has a serving maid called Lucky, who carries all her stuff. Beckett cycled tremendously when he was young, cycling and walking all over Dublin, with his Kerry blue bitch dog. He loves sports. He got his rugby pink at Trinity College and was regarded as a very good athlete in his younger days. He used to be a par four golfer but now he can't see the ball. He is fond of cricket, but he can't go to matches anymore so he watches them on his television set, which he peers at closely.

He left Trinity College where he was a professor of French and Italian. One day in the middle of teaching, the light came on: 'Why the hell am I teaching something I know nothing about?'

Sam has a hang-up on the letter M: Murphy, Malone, Molloy and the W in Watt is an inverted M. I said to him, 'Do you realise that M is the 13th letter?' He has two superstitions, one that he would not outlive his father, two that he is afraid of Friday the 13th. He was born on Good Friday, the 13th. His father was a surveyor. Sam was a highly sensitive child. His father would take him over the hills marching. At Martello Tower, the men's bathing place, from a height of 40 feet, his father pushed him off, when he was quite young. Despite his fright, swimming and walking became his favourite ways of keeping fit.

At 63, his father suddenly dropped dead. At his 63rd birthday, Sam said to me [he claps his hands], 'I outlived my father!' For an intellectual man, it is amazing he would have such superstitions.

He has China blue eyes, always subject to deterioration of sorts, the same kind of eyes that Joyce and O'Casey had. He was afraid of going blind. With O'Casey, all his life every morning Eileen had to get hot cloths and unstick his eyes. Joyce had trouble with his eyes, too. Beckett didn't until later years.

MG: Did Beckett ever meet O'Casey?

JM: He was terribly anxious to meet him. I wanted to bring them together. I wanted to be a fly on the wall when they met.

MG: Could you compare them?

JM: They were diametrically opposite. O'Casey was on a completely different plane. He was influenced by Boucicault. Beckett is influenced by Dante and Joyce. O'Casey did not agree with Beckett's philosophy, but thought he was a great writer. I love both of them, but I love Beckett by far. Beckett was terribly conscious of Joyce. When he would walk in Paris at 3 a.m., he would say, 'That's where Joyce would go.' He never was Joyce's secretary. Joyce kept everyone at arm's length. He was going blind when he was writing *Finnegans Wake*. Beckett was very young, and he would read the manuscript back to him. Joyce's daughter fell in love with Beckett. He used to take her out to tea. He was aware that she had become very emotionally involved. He told her, 'I go to your house not to see you but to see your father.' Eventually her madness became more acute and violent. She still writes to Beckett in more lucid moments. One reason he did not want to accept the Nobel Prize was that in his heart of hearts, he felt that Joyce was entitled to it for bringing a whole new scope to the English language.

MG: Why did Beckett move from Ireland to France?

JM: The repressive nature of Ireland did not permit him to do what he wanted to do. Those who had something to say could not say it. I left because I felt I had come to a dead end. Dublin was stifling me. In 1954, I became an exile. I had to start from scratch in London. In 1956 I went to Torquay and met Sean [O'Casey] and became a constant weekender there up until his death. He was a very colourful character. He could be very vicious on paper. He hated the repression going on in Ireland, but he wrote about the joy of life. This frail man, who never drank, would start singing ballads at 11 at night and go on until 3 in the morning.

I asked Sam why he wrote novels in French. He said he was afraid of our heritage, so fond of rhetorical phrases and flowery sentences. If he would write in French, then translate it, he would write three words instead of 12 words. It was the discipline. He would have to be so concise. He can put tragedy and comedy into one sentence, as in *Endgame:* 'Nothing is funnier than unhappiness I'll grant you that.' It's funny and sad, tragic and comic, in one line.

Beckett loves painters. He has a coterie of friends who join together at La Coupole or a place on rue de la Gaîté at two or three in the morning. Once he looked very tired. He just finished his work and was drained creatively. He said, 'That's the last one. Nothing more to say.'

I've never been so deeply committed to a writer as to Beckett. It was a marriage. When I started working on Fluther [in *The Plough and the Stars*], I began to notice Vladimir creeping in. This is jovial old Fluther from O'Casey suddenly turning into Vladimir.

I've given talks at colleges. The appreciation for Beckett's work so overwhelmed me. I'm going to continue to devote all my life to his writing. I've had offers to play my anthology in Papua New Guinea, Port Moresby and San Juan. In Dublin it was a great success. I haven't had one word from London to perform this show. They have their noses stuck in the old classics. But if they don't want it, they're not going to get it. I have too much respect for Beckett's work to hawk it around.

Two days later, MacGowran and I met again, and he talked about his late start in the theatre and about O'Casey, and all the other places he was taking his Beckett anthology, including Toronto, Montreal and Rome.

JM: I was an insurance policy drafter for eight years. I was doing amateur work. When I was 27 I joined the Abbey. Then I took off for France and studied mime with Étienne Decroux and with Louis Jouvet. That was in 1949. Beckett was there, but we didn't meet. Later I did *The Caretaker* and Ionesco in Dublin. I know Ionesco very well. He's basically a one-act playwright. He's a very peppery individual. He attacks critics. Sam would never attempt to criticise a critic. Ionesco is a small, bald, rotund little man, just like a comic to look at. He is bitter and sarcastic, viciously witty. But I like him very much. He and Sam are totally pole-stars. The myth about Beckett being removed in Paris is ridiculous. He must be inundated with manuscripts

The anthology started as a labour of love. It never entered my mind that it would be commercial. An anthology for my own delectation. It became a breadwinner. I can put it away and take it out again.

In the course of our meetings, I told MacGowran that I was thinking about writing a biography of Beckett. He expressed his enthusiasm for the project and offered to recommend it to the playwright. Before he finished his run in The Plough and the Stars *and before my article could be printed, MacGowran suddenly died, and the interview remained unpublished. In March, I sent Beckett a letter speaking about MacGowran and his memorial service and mentioning my interest in writing Beckett's biography. He responded from Morocco where he was on holiday:*

My life was devoid of interest – to put it mildly, and much better left unwritten. I know I have no say in the matter, except to the effect that I could be of no help to my biographer.

I expect to be around this summer and should be happy to see you then, quite privately.

That first letter from Beckett perfectly summed up his perspective on himself: forget the life, but if you want to talk, we can do it privately and not for publication. Our correspondence

27

and our missed meetings continued through the next few years. In January 1977 I reviewed three collections of Beckett, I Can't Go On, I'll Go On *and two play anthologies,* Ends and Odds *and* Fizzles. *I sent him a copy of that review and commented on his word usage, saying that I thought I knew what pizzle meant, but was puzzled by the word fizzle. In his response, he was more forthcoming than he had been in his previous letters. He offered two definitions of fizzle:*

1. The act of breaking wind quietly, i.e. an unsuccessful fart.
2. A fiasco or failure. The French 'foirade' has the same meanings, plus wetness in the literal.

Then, for my further edification (and amusement), he defined pizzle as 'a bull's penis used for flogging'. Finally, having read the book review, he commented on my use of the expression 'uproarious pessimism' to describe his philosophy:

'Uproarious pessimism' is extremely *bon trovato* [Italian for appropriate]. As Nell once said 'nothing is funnier than unhappiness.'

In 1978, he responded to a note by saying that we would be in Paris at the same time and that I should meet him in the Café Français at the Hotel PLM on Boulevard St. Jacques, near his home. Cryptically he added, 'Fear this is all I have to offer. Don't trouble to reply. I'll be there in any case.'

Conversations with Beckett

24 June 1978
'Theatre was the light.
Then it became its own darkness'

As I later learned, Beckett was a stickler for promptness. In any case, I arrived almost an hour early. I parked my car on a side street and walked along the Boulevard St. Jacques. The PLM is a modern, airline-style hotel, busy with travellers in transit. In keeping with the hotel, the Café Français is a sleekly modern café, the kind of place one would not expect to find Samuel Beckett, and therefore exactly the kind of place where one should expect to find him. He seemed to warm to the coldness and the impersonality.

Precisely at 11 a.m., I entered the café. He was already there, a tall, dour figure sitting in a far corner. He was wearing a rust-coloured tweed jacket and loose turtleneck and small round dark glasses, like Hamm. He was having an espresso and smoking a small thin black cigar. After exchanging greetings and ordering coffee, I began telling him about Frank Dunlop's recent production of *Waiting for Godot* at the Brooklyn Academy of Music. It was billed as Beckett's production, which had been done previously at BAM in German. Actually this was Dunlop's recast American version, and it was far outclassed by the German original. Clearly Beckett did not like the idea of Dunlop capitalising on his name. About 15 minutes into our discussion, I asked if I could take notes. He said, assertively, 'But this is not an interview.' And that was that. Never again in all our meetings did I suggest taking notes.

This initial conversation covered many areas, but focused to a great extent on *Waiting for Godot*. He confirmed that he had finished it in 1949 and then for the next four years tried to get it and his earlier play, *Eleutheria*, produced. Asked if he took *Waiting for Godot* around to producers, he said, 'My wife took it around. Everyone turned it down. It was like giving it to the concierge.' Then someone told him about Roger Blin, a Parisian actor and director with an affinity for the avant-garde. He saw Blin's production of Strindberg's *Ghost Sonata*, and was struck by two things: the fidelity to the author and the near emptiness of the theatre, conditions that endeared Blin to Beckett. Beckett's wife, Suzanne, gave Blin both *Waiting for Godot* and *Eleutheria*. *Eleutheria* was, Beckett said, 'a more ambitious play than *Godot*, with a bigger cast. It would have been more expensive.' He thought that was probably one reason why Blin chose *Godot*, adding in hindsight that he would not want *Eleutheria* to be staged. Later he dedicated *Endgame* to Blin 'because no one else would do *Godot*'.

Beckett did not go to the opening of *Godot* in Paris but went soon after and found it a 'thoroughly unnerving experience'. He hated to see his plays; it made him extremely nervous and self-conscious. 'I see all my mistakes,' he said. On the other hand, he liked rehearsals. At rehearsals, he could correct his mistakes.

Why did he write *Godot* in French rather than in English?

'Because English was too easy. I wanted the discipline.' Then comparing plays to fiction, he said that he liked 'the limitations of theatre as compared to the non-limitations of prose. I turned to theatre as relief – from the blackness of prose.' After fiction, 'theatre was the light.' Glumly, he added, 'Then it became its own darkness.'

He said he wrote *Godot* in four months, 'very fast, never faster', not knowing where it was going or what it was called. He wrote it in French in an exercise book, first page to last. When he reached the end of the notebook, he said, he turned it over and continued writing on the reverse side of the pages, back to front. There were some corrections and emendations, but no pages torn out. Illustrating the process, he took the check from the café table, folded it in half and, almost as if he were performing a card trick, he flipped it over. At the gesture, the waiter scurried over, thinking we wanted to settle the bill. Beckett and I both smiled at the waiter's mistake, and Beckett tried to explain to him that he was using the check in a demonstration. With a helpless shrug, he gave up the attempt, and we ordered more coffee.

After he finished the play in longhand, he typed it. 'I still have the manuscript,' he said. Apparently it was one of the few he retained. At first, Gogo was named Levy. He said he didn't know why he changed the name, except that he wanted the two names to be a definite contrast: Didi and Gogo. 'They are players,' he said. 'They play games,' as do Pozzo and Lucky. 'They are role players,' in other words, actors. 'Pozzo need not be a plutocrat. Blin had him played that way, but Pozzo is also a player,' and in common with the other characters, 'he runs out of games to play.'

I asked him about Lucky's monologue. He said it could be divided into three clear parts. The first, which ends 'but not so fast', is about 'heaven and divine aphasia'.The second, which begins 'and considering what is more', is about 'man, who is shrinking'. The third, which begins 'considering what is more, much more grave', is about 'the earth below, the earth abode of stones'. Then he said, 'Lucky plays at the game of being intellectual.' His aim is to be 'a good bearer'.

He had not seen the original American production, but heard about it through Alan Schneider, who had been fired 'after the Miami fiasco' and replaced by Herbert Berghof. About Bert Lahr, he said, 'He made *Godot* about him.' I said I had seen the play on Broadway and that Lahr had been very much in character, and was also very funny.

The talk turned to his other plays. He confirmed that he had written *Krapp's Last Tape* for Patrick Magee. Although he didn't know him at the time, he had heard him on the radio and liked the sound of his voice. 'That was really the only time I wrote directly for anyone.' He added that when Albert Finney played Krapp in a revival in London, he was 'hopeless; he had as much poetry as an ashtray.' With *Happy Days*, Beckett returned to writing in English because he felt he was 'losing' the language.

He said that he felt his titles suffered in translation, in both directions. *Fin de partie* was better than *Endgame*, because *Endgame* 'means only chess; "Fin de partie" could be any game. Chess is important to the play, but it is not the only game suggested by it.' *Footfalls* is untranslatable into French, and *That Time* 'is worse; it becomes "L'Occasion." It loses the double meaning. "Pas moi" [for *Not I*] is literal.'

Was the inspiration for *Not I* seeing a mother and child in Algiers?

'The inspiration was a Caravaggio painting that I saw in Malta, of John the Baptist's head.' Reluctantly, he revealed, 'Also in North Africa: I saw a mother waiting for a child to come out of school. The idea of someone watching the watcher.' Then, about *Footfalls*, he said, 'It is about the pacing: nine steps one way, nine steps the other. The fall of feet. The sound of feet. Walking on the ground, as on a tomb. The words are less important, but they are essential.'

At that moment, his writing was at a standstill. 'I'm not writing now. I'm trying to write prose, but not every day. It's difficult.' At least momentarily, he was concentrating on directing, both in Germany and in London (soon he was to direct Billie Whitelaw in *Happy Days*). Explaining why he had not gone to the theatre in years, he said, 'I lost the appetite. As a young man, I saw everything at the Abbey: O'Casey, Synge.' He liked early O'Casey, especially *Juno and the Paycock*. 'Mrs. O'Casey is now at this hotel,' he said, indicating that he knew her but had never met her husband.

He had lost his appetite for other arts, like painting, attributing that partly to his eye problem: he had had two operations for cataracts. Sports on television remained a primary interest. Faithfully he watched the World Cup and tennis, and we spoke briefly about both. In this and future meetings, tennis was to prove a frequent topic of conversation.

Speaking about his earlier years, he said that when he graduated from Trinity College in Dublin he had planned to be a teacher. He tried that profession but 'decided it was hopeless. I was teaching what I didn't know to people who didn't want to learn.' Was that like directing actors? 'No!' At that point, he had written 'the odd poem, like everyone else', but had not yet decided to be a writer. Did he regret not being a teacher? 'Sometimes,' he said, indicating that one of the attractions had been the regular pay – and the time off. But as a writer he can determine his own schedule, and take a vacation or a journey whenever he wanted to. 'No. Never! Not even when I'm not writing.' Then he announced, 'I became a writer, because all else failed.'

For years, Harold Pinter had sent him manuscripts of his plays, and he would respond with comments. 'He always sends me his plays. I read his new one, *Betrayal*. I liked it. It's about an affair. It works from the end of an affair backwards to the beginning.' He admitted that, in other respects, he was out of touch with theatre but was curious about Edward Albee. He had seen Schneider's production of *Who's Afraid of Virginia Woolf?* in London. Many plays are sent to him by young writers; he is unable to read them. He asked about the Mabou Mines and listened as I described how the company had dramatised *Cascando* and *The Lost Ones*, which became a tour de force for David Warrilow. He said to say hello to Warrilow should I see him.

How did he feel about the Bair biography? He almost trembled in response, averting his eyes and shaking off the entire notion. 'There is nothing to say about it' – in other words, it was a closed book. At one point, deep into the conversation, he said, 'I'm tired of talking about my work.' I took that in the broadest sense, not only that he was weary of talking to me about a specific play, but that he did not want to talk to anyone about any of his work. He seemed to mean that not just for the present but forever.

22 June 1979

'Directing is an excuse not to write'

The next year, the situation repeated itself: we met in the morning and talked over a double espresso. He looked somewhat more gaunt, and his eyes seemed strained.

Beckett spoke about his production of *Happy Days* with Billie Whitelaw. It began with Winnie sleeping; he demonstrated her position on stage by putting his arm under his head. Then the lights came up. He said that Billie at first had problems because she was following other actresses in the role. With *Footfalls*, she had created the role. But with the author's help, she left her own imprint on *Happy Days* as well. In the end, he said, 'she became darker, in voice, not in terms of light,' and she was sexy. Coincidentally, Irene Worth was playing *Happy Days* at the Public Theatre in New York. I told him that she had compared Winnie to Chaplin's tramp in terms of her 'marvellous resilience'. She had also said, 'I'm shy about going all out, but I have to do what Beckett wants. Just throw caution to the wind!'

For Beckett, rehearsals in London were arduous. He had prepared for it far in advance. This would be, he vowed, the last play of his that he would direct. Up to then, he had directed them all, 'but not all in English'. Directing, he decided, took him away from his writing. 'Directing is an excuse not to write.' He wanted to record more things 'on white paper'.

In casting the production he had interviewed seven actors for the role of Winnie's husband, Willie. He chose Leonard Fenton at least partly because he was also a singer and sang Schubert. During breaks in rehearsal, he cheered Beckett with his singing. 'It's a hard part, Willie. The actor has to be very

adept. It allows for improvisations.' He praised the set design.
It was 'not really a mound, just an incline. It's somewhat
misleading to call it a mound.' I asked him to compare Billie
Whitelaw's performance to Madeleine Renaud's, and he said,
apologetically, that Renaud was 'sentimental'.

Each time he staged a play, this and others, the play
changed. While directing, he found 'superfluities: words as
well as actions'. He pointed to *Endgame* as an example: 'Clov
climbs up the ladder, looks out, then gets down and forgets to
move the ladder. I cut that.' But that was funny. You cut a
laugh? He laughed at the thought.

He had been working on two new pieces, 'a dramatic
monologue for David Warrilow' (*A Piece of Monologue*) and
a narrative fragment. The monologue began 'when David said
he wanted to talk about death for an hour.' As it developed,
the piece was about 'a man in white under a lamp; the man
and the lamp were parallel.' After writing the piece, he put it
away until Martin Esslin said the Kenyon Review was being
revived and asked Beckett if he had something that could be
included in an issue. He sent him *A Piece of Monologue*.

The narrative was begun 'to keep me company', but he
gave it up after writing 10,000 words 'because it was not
good company.' He described it: 'A man is lying on his back
in the dark. He hears a voice giving him a past which he will
not accept. Who is the voice, what is the past? This may be
one man keeping himself company.' He said he might go
back to writing it. Entitled *Company*, the narrative was
performed the following year by Patrick Magee on BBC
radio, and later in New York by the Mabou Mines.

When Beckett was in London, he had seen Nicol
Williamson. In 1964 Williamson had appeared as Didi in
Waiting for Godot at the Royal Court, with MacGowran as
Lucky. Beckett had liked Williamson and, still harping on
Finney, he said, with regret, that he could have had
Williamson instead of Finney in *Krapp's Last Tape*.

He reiterated that he didn't go to the theatre because he
hated to sit in an audience. He felt trapped. As with *Happy*

Days, he stayed with the play through rehearsal, then did not see it with an audience.

Next week he was going to his country house in Ussy. He hadn't been there since January, and in July he was planning to go to Morocco. He always stayed at the same hotel and spent much of his time swimming. There were, he said, beautiful beaches in Morocco. We talked about Arrabal, whom he hadn't seen lately, and Ionesco. He said that *La Cantatrice Chauve* [*The Bald Soprano* or *Prima Donna*] was still playing in Paris after 20 years. *The Mousetrap* of Paris? He laughed at the thought.

At that point, he tried to pay the check, saying, 'You can pay when I come to New York.' 'When is that?', I asked. Of course, he had no intention of going to New York. He had been been there once, for the filming of *Film* with Buster Keaton, and clearly that had been enough. He suddenly announced that he had to go on an errand. We left the café together and he headed toward the Santé prison. I wondered if he were visiting someone there.

Later that day, he mailed me a copy of *A Piece of Monologue*, which he had typed single space in one paragraph over four pages. In the margin were his precise proofreading marks, correcting misspellings, inserting several new words and changing a question mark to a period.

4 July 1982

'Were a woman to do it, it would be like having a soprano sing a baritone role'

As I entered the PLM, I saw Beckett leaving the newsstand. He had purchased a copy of the Daily Telegraph and asked if I wanted one. We walked into the café together. He was relatively cheerful, if one could ever use that word about Beckett.

He had written two new pieces: the play, *Catastrophe*, for Václav Havel, to be presented at the Avignon Festival, and a television play sent to Stuttgart. Along with Arthur Miller, Eugène Ionesco and Max Frisch, he had been asked to write a piece for Havel, whom he greatly admired. Because the play was for a French festival, he wrote it in French. He said it was short, about 15 minutes, and it was pronounced *Catastroph*, without the final e, the way it is in Greek, meaning the end. He expressed a certain concern about the television play. He had not yet heard from Stuttgart. He thought the play might be rejected. Beckett worrying about rejection? It was a voice-less play, inspired by a Schubert piece he played at his house in the country. It was 'about endings'. Several years before, he had written a dance piece for Stuttgart. If the new piece was done, he would go to Stuttgart and 'snoop around'. Entitled *Quad*, a 'piece for four players, light and percussion', it was performed in Stuttgart in October and in December on BBC-2.

When he directs, he is on stage with the actors, contrary to the German method where the director sits in the audience 'and gives orders'. Once again, he said he did not plan to direct: it was 'too demanding'.

The talk turned to *Krapp's Last Tape*. He reiterated that it had been written for Patrick Magee, who was the definitive

Krapp. There had been many requests for actresses to play the role. Naturally he had refused. 'It should always be played by a man,' he said. 'It's a man's voice. Were a woman to do it, it would be like having a soprano sing a baritone role.' Then he asked, if a woman played the role, 'What do you do about the scene in the boat?', Krapp's romantic recollection. I suggested that it would become a lesbian romance. He laughed at the idea. There had also been requests for an all-female *Godot* and a female Hamm in *Endgame*. He would have none of it. A request from Germany for a female *Godot* came to him after the play had gone into rehearsal and was about to open. Still he rejected it.

The Japanese Noh theatre wanted to do *Rockaby* and *Ohio Impromptu* at the Edinburgh Festival. He gave his approval but insisted that it be done 'only in Japanese'. He had been told that he was influenced by Noh. His response: he had never seen Noh. He was angry that Billie Whitelaw was having difficulty performing in America, that Actors Equity had raised some objection. He called it a 'banning'.

Acting as his agent, Barney Rosset 'arranges things', such as the sale of *Catastrophe* to the New Yorker. Speaking about Rosset, he said that Joan Mitchell, who had an exhibition on at the time, was Rosset's first wife. He seemed amused by the fact that his friend had been married four times.

He spoke about other friends, including Martin Segal, whom he had met through Henry Wenning. Wenning had worked with Segal in his actuarial company. Wenning was also a book collector. Beckett had sold him manuscripts when he 'was hard up'. Beckett and Segal always met when Segal was in Paris. He remembered meeting Athol Fugard in the pub next to the Royal Court in London. Fugard told him he smoked a Cap and Peterson, a pipe referred to in *Waiting for Godot*. Beckett said he did not know Fugard's plays. I talked about them, especially *Boesman and Lena*, and its debt to *Godot*. Recently, Herbert Mitgang, a colleague and friend of mine at the New York Times, had written a piece about

Beckett in the Times, and Beckett was angry about it. He said it had been done through false pretences. Mitgang had seen him 'for personal reasons' and not for an interview. As a comment on the writer's behaviour, Beckett offered a pun: 'I will never Mitgang with him again.'

Talking about Alan Schneider's film, *Film*, he said that Buster Keaton had accepted the role simply as 'a job'. That was your last visit to New York, I said. 'My only visit', he said with finality. It was unbearably hot, he recalled. Keaton did not know Beckett's plays. They could only talk about silent movies. Still Beckett seemed to like him, perhaps largely in memory of Keaton's comedy.

Disgruntled, Beckett said he spent too much time on his mail, answering requests for rights and for him to read manuscripts. When he was a young man, he said, he would never send manuscripts to other writers. He did not have a secretary, even for his own manuscripts. First he wrote in longhand, then he typed them, using the hunt and peck system, which he demonstrated by fingering the air. Things change between longhand and typing; the typewriter was his 'friend'. I suggest, 'collaborator'.

Would he have liked to have seen Laurel and Hardy in *Godot*? He seemed tantalised by the idea. They were 'ideal physically', he said. Young actors have imitated the Marx Brothers, I said, why not Laurel and Hardy? Then he said, 'It's too late,' meaning they were dead. I spoke about Bill Irwin and other new American clowns, and that sparked his interest.

Had he ever acted? 'Once, in school. In Corneille's *El Cid*. I played El Viejo, the old man. The beginning and end of my acting career. We called the play *El Kid*.' Would he ever want to play Krapp? 'I couldn't work the recorder,' he said conclusively.

As a devotee of tennis, and a vigorous player in his youth, he was fascinated by the rivalry between Chris Evert and Martina Navratilova. He said he liked Evert's 'humanity', and thought Navratilova 'manly'.

When I arrived in London several days later, there was a copy of *Catastrophe* waiting for me, in Beckett's English translation. The following January the play appeared in the New Yorker.

24 June 1983

'No idea'

Wearing sneaker-like shoes and a jacket over a pullover shirt, he looked as if he might have been jogging. He seemed spry. We met in the lobby and walked into the café where he immediately lit a cigar with a lighter that was inscribed with the name Wolfgang. I asked him about it, and he said absentmindedly that he did not know where the lighter came from.

Schneider had sent him my review of three one-act plays, *Catastrophe*, *Ohio Impromptu* and *What Where*, which opened earlier that month at the Harold Clurman Theatre in New York. Beckett thanked me for the review but said he disagreed with one point. I had written that at the end of *Catastrophe*, David Warrilow seemed to be 'appealing' to his audience. What I had written was: 'We are left, finally with a spectral tableau: a martyr, raising his head, fixing his audience in his gaze and staring in abject supplication.' Although he had not seen the performance, Beckett knew of course what he had intended: 'It was a look of overcoming, of cowing his audience into submission, of causing the applause to die.'

He praised Warrilow, though he had not seen him in either *Catastrophe* or *Ohio Impromptu*. About *What Where*, he said, 'I don't know what it means. Don't ask me what it means. It's an object.' I suggested that it might be a dream. He suggested that it might be 'about a place without issue. No exit. The four [Bam, Bom, Bim, Bem] are trapped. One by one they have an opportunity to ask the victim what where, and they receive no answer. If they did, perhaps they would leave.' He said that Jean-Louis Barrault was going to do *Catastrophe* in September, and seemed curious at the prospect.

Later when we talked about Giacometti, the feeling of the play was re-evoked. For Giacometti, 'things were insolvable, but that kept him going,' as if art derived from an inability to find solutions. Giacometti was a friend of his, but not 'a good friend'. They would meet at cafés and go to the artist's studio. Asked if he ever posed for him, Beckett seemed surprised at the question, and replied in the negative.

A new prose piece, *Worstward Ho*, had just been published. It was about 10,000 words (after our meeting he sent me a copy), and he had written nothing since. 'No idea,' he said. What did he do when he was not working? 'Who knows?' One thing he does is watch television. He had just seen Gerulaitis beat Krishna, and he had read in that day's paper about McEnroe's latest tantrum.

He had been in London in December for *Rockaby*, which Billie Whitelaw had done at the National Theatre. Schneider had directed her. Uncharacteristically, Beckett had gone to the opening night party. He said that he liked Schneider because he was 'very careful and scrupulous' in his directing. Schneider had sent him the London reviews of *Rockaby*, and when I asked about them, Beckett shrugged them off. I said, perhaps they expected something else from him. He gave a look that said, 'Ah, well.'

When I talked about Tennessee Williams, he said he liked A *Streetcar Named Desire* and other early plays. Then he asked about his friend, Israel Horovitz. I spoke about Sam Shepard and Lanford Wilson and how reportedly Shepard had been out of town and 'phoned in' his direction of his play, *Fool for Love*, Off-Broadway. He seemed fascinated by the idea of a playwright as absentee director.

An assistant to Andrzej Wajda was doing two Beckett fragments in Paris. Beckett had given his permission because the director needed it 'in order to stay in France'. Beckett thought they were still being performed and wrote the name of the theatre on a napkin for me.

The conversation rambled into politics. He said he disliked Margaret Thatcher's voice but was interested in Reagan as a communicator. He seemed stirred by the Pope and his vitality especially after the recent assassination attempt. He said he thought the Pope would have liked to remain in Poland. I said that he had once wanted to be a playwright, and Beckett added that he had also wanted to be an actor. A failed playwright and actor becomes Pope, a failed actor becomes President – what did he think of that? He mused about it, but offered no response.

Arrabal had told me about what he called 'the Paris school' with himself, Ionesco, Genet and Beckett as prominent members, saying that they would occasionally meet. Although Beckett shunned the idea of a school of writers, he admitted that they all knew each other and were working in Paris at the same time. He expressed his admiration for Arrabal, especially for his political activism and his bravery. Recently there was a large Communist anti-nuclear march in Paris. Everyone carried anti-American signs, except for Arrabal, who boldly carried an anti-Russian sign. For that reason, other demonstrators attacked him. Beckett watched the event on television.

At the end of the year, there was a brief exchange of greetings. I sent him a photograph I had taken of him and asked him if he would sign it, and I expressed my relief that Billie Whitelaw had at last been recognised as an actress of 'international stature', and was being allowed to perform *Rockaby*, *Footfalls* and *Enough* Off-Broadway. He responded in January with a picture postcard labelled 'La Belle Époque', showing two overdressed Victorian ladies and a young girl digging a sand castle. He wrote: 'Forgive this brief response. I am destroyed with mail.'

On 3 May Alan Schneider was struck by a motorcycle while crossing the street in London, and died.

Later that month, as a member of the New York Drama Critics Circle, I suggested that a special citation be given to Beckett for his body of work, including the two evenings of one-acts presented that season. It was the first time that his work had been acknowledged by the Critics Circle. In response, Beckett wrote from Paris:

Dear Drama Critics
Thank you for your cable.
I am greatly touched by this high mark of your esteem and send you my most sincere gratitude.

29 June 1984
'My last gasp'

Sitting in my car waiting for the time of our appointment, I thought of things we might talk about: Brian Bedford's *Waiting for Godot*; Schneider's death and his memorial service; Billie Whitelaw and her fluttering hands conducting a performance; the long run in New York of Beckett's six one-acts; the Beckett Society meeting at the Modern Language Association.

After a most cordial greeting, he asked me to call him Sam (and I, of course, asked him to return the informality). He looked fit, but said he was not well, facing 'the old familiar: disaster, misery, extremity'. I noticed for the first time that a finger on his right hand seemed permanently arched, the result of a muscular condition. He had cancelled a planned trip to Stuttgart in May for a television version of *Worstward Ho*.

Devastated by Schneider's death, he said he couldn't imagine anyone else directing his work in America. A call came in the morning from Jocelyn Herbert in London. Schneider had been working at the Hampstead Theatre and had gone out to post a letter; after he had mailed it, he was struck by a motorcycle. The next day Beckett received that letter. It was about their upcoming meeting in Paris. Because this was probably Schneider's last letter, Beckett seemed to feel partly responsible for his death.

He had read my piece in the Times about Schneider's memorial, and we talked about George Grizzard's affectionate anecdote about the director. Schneider had been angry at the actor for arriving two minutes late for a rehearsal of *The Country Girl*. In response, Schneider had walked out, then had come back in a fury and thrown his script into the air. In the play, Grizzard was playing a director not unlike Schneider, and he casually asked him if he could use this bit of directorial 'business' in the play. Beckett was amused by the story, adding that Schneider 'took such painstaking care with his work', though they did not always agree on details. In contrast, there was Peter Hall, who directed the first English *Godot* with 'a cluttered stage'. Beckett also expressed dissatisfaction with Peter Bull's Pozzo in that production.

Pinter had sent him a copy of *One for the Road*. Pinter, he said, was 'obsessed with threats to freedom'. Beckett read both that play and *A Kind of Alaska*, and liked them.

He said that when Billie Whitelaw finished her run in *Rockaby* in New York, there was talk (mostly from Jack Garfein) about replacing her with Katharine Hepburn. 'Leave Hepburn,' Beckett advised Garfein, 'and let Billie return,' which she was to do in January 'after making money elsewhere.' He praised her as 'an instinctive actress'. He was surprised, and, of course, pleased, by the long run of the one-acts. The first three, with Warrilow and Alvin Epstein, were on their way to Edinburgh and then to London.

We talked about James Joyce and the new revised version of *Ulysses* correcting the supposed 5000 errors in the novel. He blamed the mistakes on the printers more than on the typist. Although Joyce supposedly read proof, his eyes were so bad that 'he couldn't read.' He said that Joyce dictated parts of *Finnegans Wake* to him. Did he edit it or change anything? 'No,' he said with a hint of a smile. I said, perhaps there will also be a new version of *Finnegans Wake*, correcting 10,000 errors. I had recently read Robert McAlmon's *Being Geniuses Together* (about Joyce, Hemingway and McAlmon, among others). His comment: 'Joyce said that was the Office Boy's Revenge.'

Before going to Paris from Dublin for the first time, Beckett had read *A Portrait of the Artist as a Young Man* and *Dubliners*, and had heard about the work on *Ulysses*. He was 22 when he arrived in Paris. It was, in all respects, a great experience for him, although he was confronted by 'warring camps'. 'The Surrealists, André Breton, laying down the law – the artistic law; and Joyce had his own circle: Mary Reynolds, Nancy Cunard. Sylvia Beach was very nice to me.' He said he met Hemingway at Shakespeare and Company and Hemingway referred to Joyce as 'the old boy'. Beckett had read Hemingway's early short stories and *A Farewell to Arms*, but never really liked the man. On the other hand he enjoyed Marcel Duchamp, who lived near him. I commented on Duchamp's found objects, such as the urinal he exhibited as a work of art. Beckett laughed: 'A writer could not do that.'

He said that Giacometti and his brother were close, but one was subordinate to the other, 'like the van Goghs'. Speaking of siblings, he said that the van Veldes, Geer and Bram, were unfriendly to one another. He was friends with both of them, but liked Bram's art more.

On his own work: *Worstward Ho* was his last, and he had not written anything since. That was, he said, 'my last gasp'. Other last gasps were to follow.

He hadn't been to his country house in some time, but thought he might go soon. He usually went by train. 'My wife doesn't like the country. I go by myself.' Once there, he drives his car, a 20-year-old Citroen 2CV. It was, he said, 'old, battered and a great friend'. He used to ride a bicycle, but gave it up, and now stayed with his 2CV. His house is isolated, but there are nearby stores for provisions. He likes 'the silence'.

In Paris he has had two apartments. He moved to his present home on Boulevard St. Jacques because he liked the open air and the trees. He said his home was surrounded by 'the madhouse, the hospital and the prison'. Quoting David Mamet, I said that he would be prepared 'if God forbid, the inevitable should occur.' I told him about being awakened two nights before by a loud noise, and he said, immediately, that it was shouting when France won the football championship.

He said that Sam Shepard was having a busy Paris season, and I told him that Shepard was also a movie star, that his acting supported his playwriting: an artist's dream. Beckett was surprised and quite taken with the idea. 'As an actor?' he asked.

Having seen Brian Bedford as Didi in *Waiting for Godot* at the Stratford Festival in Ontario, I described the unusual way he performed the 'idle discourse' scene, climbing on top of Pozzo's case, as if he were mounting a soapbox. He said that Pozzo and Lucky should be lying down, and Didi should walk around them. But he was interested in Bedford's approach and did not object. He said he would have to be careful about his footing.

He recalled that the first time he saw Rick Cluchey in *Godot*, he played Pozzo. He said that Cluchey was putting together a repertory of *Godot* and *Krapp's Last Tape*, and would tour Australia.

I asked him how his papers had gotten to the University of Texas. He said that after the war when he needed money, 'Jake Schwartz, the Great Extractor', bought manuscripts at a low price. Explaining his choice of epithet, he said that Schwartz was also a dentist. According to Beckett, he 'plundered' him and other artists and then sold things for a high price to Texas. Beckett liked Carlton Lake, the head of the Texas archives, but mocked Schwartz. On letters: 'you send them, unprepared for posterity, and then people sell them. The rights to the letters belong to the writer, but the letters are available to others and people write about them.'

In passing, he said that he still had an original copy of *Ulysses* but didn't know where it was.

He did not seem aware of the Mabou Mines production of *Imagination Dead Imagine*, and I described it to him. He listened, without comment. Israel Horovitz had been in Paris and he and Beckett had met for a drink. He said that Horovitz had told him about problems he had with Burgess Meredith in a production of his play *Park Your Car in Harvard Yard*. Apparently, Meredith had difficulty remembering his lines. When I said he was a good actor, Beckett agreed, but refused to acknowledge the *Godot* that Meredith and Zero Mostel did for television. Accidentally he pronounced *Godot* with the accent on the second syllable, and then immediately corrected himself.

I asked him if he wanted another coffee. He said, 'No, but you can, Mel.' He seemed to like the sound of my name, saying it mellifluously, the way Krapp says 'spool'.

In December of that year I went to the American Repertory Theatre in Cambridge, Mass. to review JoAnne Akalaitis's production of *Endgame*, which had become a subject of conflict between Beckett and Robert Brustein, the artistic director of A.R.T. Encouraged by Barney Rosset, Beckett had objected to the production on the grounds that it disregarded his published stage directions. At his request, a note was inserted in the programme: 'Any production of *Endgame* which ignores my stage directions is completely unacceptable to me.' Such a production, he said, would be a parody. 'My play requires an empty room and two small windows.' In Akalaitis's production, the set simulated an abandoned subway station. Beckett had also objected to the use of music (an overture and background music by Philip Glass) but had allowed the production to go on. Despite the controversy, I felt that the director was respectful of the text and, all things considered, this was a fairer, though highly volatile, representation of the play than many productions I had seen. I sent a letter to Beckett to that effect.

2 July 1985

'I've gagged myself. Life's ambition'

Same as before. Beckett looked thinner: bony and gaunt. He was wearing a light grey poplin or cotton suit, neatly buttoned. He had been trying to translate *Worstward Ho* into French and was having extreme difficulty. 'I can't translate it,' he confessed. 'I can't translate the first word.' [He meant the title.] With an urgency, he said, 'I've gagged myself,' then added in a moment of Beckettian humour, 'Life's ambition.' This depressing thought set the tone for our conversation.

He was not writing anything and had not written anything for the past year. He had nothing to say. His summary of the year: 'dreary'. Momentarily he was buoyed by his work in Stuttgart. Stuttgart 'sustained' him. He flew there with some frequency. It took one hour; he always stayed at the same hotel, near the television studio, outside of the city. He hated the modern part of Stuttgart and 'a terrible new museum, designed by a Scottish architect'. Every day he would walk from the hotel up a hill to the television studio. Nearby is a favourite park where he feeds the squirrels. The studio is very up to date. He did a television version of *What Where*, working for 10 days on a film that would last about 10 minutes. It was 'reconceived for television'. He worked on the editing as well as the performance. The work was mostly 'distilling, cutting, cutting, cutting'. The production was 'more sophisticated' than *Film*. Recalling once again that Buster Keaton did not know his plays, he said that he 'worked hard and ran hard, despite the heat'. He said that Keaton told him he improvised his movie scripts. The actor 'loosened up' when they ate at a fish restaurant during a break in the shooting. Would he like to have *Film* filmed again? Yes, but there were no offers. He knew that the original did not please Keaton fans.

I said that Dustin Hoffman was interested in doing *Godot*. He replied that Jack Garfein had also told him that, too, but he didn't think that Garfein had Hoffman's agreement. I talked about the actor's virtuosity and said he would be a good Gogo. Beckett said that if the production were to go ahead, he would like Walter Asmus to direct it, or at least to be a consultant, but didn't think Hoffman would agree. I suggested Bill Irwin as Didi to Hoffman's Gogo.

He had briefly looked in at a production of *Company* in Paris and at Barrault's *Catastrophe* and liked both. Frederick Neumann from the Mabou Mines wanted to do an adaptation of *Worstward Ho*. 'I don't know,' said Beckett, reiterating his early statement, 'I can't even translate it.' I talked about Akalaitis's *Endgame*, saying she was experienced at doing his work. He said, knowledgeably, 'Yes, but adaptations not plays.'

The text of Jack MacGowran's evening of Beckett was being published and there was talk about reviving it on stage, but he said, 'Jackie's widow wants to direct or produce it.' There were too many obstacles. She had no legal rights over the text, but he felt that she had a moral right. He said he would love to see Warrilow do it. He admired the actor's bilingual talent; he had done *Catastrophe* and *A Piece of Monologue* in French. News from Rick Cluchey: the actor who played Lucky in Cluchey's *Godot*, whom Beckett said was the best Lucky he had ever seen, died of AIDS.

An Irish group had made a film about Beckett's work, the same people who had made a film for Joyce's centenary. They interviewed people who knew Beckett. Warrilow read his words, but Beckett did not appear in it.

He had been watching Wimbledon and commented on the fact that McEnroe was not in good form, and then talked about the relative merits of Boris Becker and Henri Leconte. John Lloyd had lost. 'It's easy to beat Lloyd', I said. 'Chris Evert Lloyd could beat John Lloyd,' he said.

We talked about hijackings and bombings, and the fact that the Irish wanted to plant bombs in English resorts. Was there any hope for a settlement? 'Get the British out of Ireland,' he said, matter of factly.

My wife and I had just taken a trip through the Loire Valley. He said the Loire was his first exposure to France when he was in his 20's. He rode a bicycle along the banks of the Loire. 'Did you see Amboise?' he asked, and said that it was one of his favourite chateaux.

Before I left, I took out a recent collection of his short pieces. He thumbed through it until he arrived at the script for *Film*. He pointed to the spot where he had diagrammed the placement of the dog and the cat. Recalling the difficulty, he said, 'They were more trouble than Keaton.' He signed the book, 'For Mel, from his friend Sam.'

On 11 August 1985, my wife and I went to a singular event: a private, one-time-only reading of *Waiting for Godot* in Mike Nichols's apartment in Manhattan. It was hoped that it would lead to a production celebrating Beckett's 80th birthday. Gathered in the director's living room in a penthouse in the Carlyle Hotel overlooking Central Park was an all-star cast. Dustin Hoffman (who had invited us) played Gogo and Brian Bedford was Didi. Vincent Gardenia read Pozzo (replacing José Ferrer, who was supposed to play the role) and John Malkovich was Lucky, with Glenne Headly (who was then married to Malkovich) as the Boy. Nichols directed and Jack Garfein read the stage directions. Years ago, Nichols had played Lucky in Chicago and, he said, he still remembered his lines. Guests included Gerald Schoenfeld (president of the Shubert Organisation) and his wife; Hoffman's wife Lisa; Gregory Mosher, head of Lincoln Centre Theatre. There was even a designer, Tony Walton, in the house.

The apartment was a glamourous setting for any play and a most unusual one for *Godot*. While waiting for everyone to arrive, we talked about Beckett and other matters. Having played Didi at the Stratford Festival in Canada the previous season, Bedford exuded authority. Hoffman had played Pozzo years ago in Boston and has always cherished the fact that he was able to lead Robert Duvall, his Lucky, on a rope. As usual, he had done considerable preparation, even to getting a tape of the original Broadway production. I had talked to Hoffman several days before. While he was helping to edit the film version of *Death of a Salesman*, which he had performed on Broadway, he listened to Lahr's performance in *Godot* on a Walkman.

The actors were seated, with scripts in hand, but it was far from a cold reading. They had deeply immersed themselves in the roles. In all respects, it was a remarkable evening. Hoffman's earthy humour was a splendid match for Bedford's seedy elegance. Between them there was a sense of playful rivalry, which succeeded in enhancing and equalising the relationship. They warmed to each other as vaudeville partners. Delivering Lucky's monologue, Malkovich projected a matter-of-fact madness, and Headly's touching delivery of the boy's messages from Godot might have made the author rethink his interdiction on women playing male roles. Only Gardenia seemed not entirely comfortable in his role. It was a marvellous reading and a celebratory evening.

Afterwards, Hoffman said it had been a privilege to participate, a feeling that, I think, was shared by everyone in the room. Then he told an anecdote about I.B. Singer being courted by a Hollywood producer who wanted to film one of his novels. Singer, who had just won the Nobel Prize, said, 'Do it, do it now. I'm hot!' The suggestion was that the participants in the reading were hot, along with Beckett, and Nichols should do the production now.

The next day, Nichols and I talked about the projected production. He said he wanted Hoffman and Bedford, either Malkovich or John Gielgud as Lucky (I suggested David Warrilow, if they were unavailable) and George C. Scott as Pozzo – and Glenne Headly as the Boy, which he knew would upset Beckett. If the production had come to fruition, it would have been the first time that Nichols and Hoffman had worked together since *The Graduate* in 1967, and it would have represented a fascinating blending of theatrical traditions. Unfortunately, the production ended that evening, primarily because of the actors' unavailability. It was several years before Nichols did *Godot*, at Lincoln Centre, as planned, but it was to be with an entirely different cast (Steve Martin, Robin Williams, F. Murray Abraham and Bill Irwin). But for the moment there was enthusiasm in the air.

In a letter to Beckett, I described the reading and said that the production would give *Godot* the American platform it had always deserved. Beckett replied, thanking me for my 'encouraging account' of the reading. He added, 'I look forward to meeting Dustin Hoffman here next month. David Warrilow as Lucky would be fine with me.'

In November I mailed him a copy of my New Yorker Profile of Bill Irwin, introducing him as a very talented clown-actor-mime with a particular affinity for Beckett's work. Beckett read the Profile 'with much interest', and said about Irwin, 'I have heard from him & replied that I wd. be happy to meet him in Paris. It occurs to me now that he might be interested in *Act Without Words 1* (from Grove Press edition of the shorter plays).'

In his life as in his work, Beckett was surrounded by unhappiness – by the death of relatives and friends, by his own brush with mortality in 1938 when he was inexplicably stabbed on a Paris street and by his growing debilitation. Seeing him over a period of years, one could feel his anger at the aging process. On 26 February 1986, in anticipation of his upcoming 80th birthday on 13 April, I sent him a letter asking if he might have something to say, publicly, for a piece I was going to write about that milestone. In response, he sent me a picture postcard of Paris in 1740, a scene of boats pulling up to the land adjoining the Hôtel de Ville. Unsurprisingly, he wrote, 'I have nothing to say about the sad unevent and its sad effects – for publication or otherwise. Forgive.' To have said anything else would not have been Beckettian.

Dutifully, I wrote a piece on his birthday, explaining that he declined to comment, and quoting one of his rare published statements on art: 'There is nothing to express, nothing with which to express, together with the obligation to express.' In this case, he had been speaking about painting, but the words echoed through his own work as playwright and novelist.

My piece continued:

Ineluctably drawn to his destiny like one of his own wanderers doomed to ambulate in a closeted void, Beckett has kept writing, producing a body of work that is unmatched for its density, specificity and artistic influence. As we celebrate his 80th birthday, it is evident that Beckett is the pre-eminent playwright of his time and one of the foremost experimental novelists.

The themes that have preoccupied him for more than half a century instil all of his art, and, one might add, his waking and dreaming lives. At 80, Beckett is both an icon of his age and an emblem of survivability. If Beckett can go on, perhaps we can follow.

On his birthday, Beckett was honoured throughout the world. That week in New York, there were almost daily lectures and panels analysing his art. In Paris, there was a city-wide festival of Beckett plays as well as a four-day symposium with 30 Beckett specialists gathered to deliver papers on subjects as varied as 'Beckett and St. Francis of Assisi' and 'Beckett, Yeats and Noh'. In the U.S., there was one major national event: National Public Radio broadcast *All That Fall*, with Everett Frost directing an all-star Beckett cast (Billie Whitelaw, David Warrilow, Alvin Epstein, Jerome Kilty).

30 June 1987

'Every other line a laugh?'

I caught up with Beckett in the lobby of the hotel. Nattily attired in jacket and tie, he looked sporty, and I told him so. 'I don't feel sporty,' he said. From the first, he sounded glum. Clearly not everything was right with him. The café was almost empty. Trying to cheer him up, I began talking about tennis, and he admitted to a sneaking fondness for Jimmy Connors and an admiration for Steffi Graf. I told him my wife and I were going to the Dordogne and asked if he had ever been there. He said no but had heard that it was a place of great scenic beauty. Soon the conversation turned to his work. He said he was not working on anything, not even a piece for German television. He wanted to work again in Stuttgart, but had no idea. *Ohio Impromptu* had been suggested; he thought not.

I knew he had seen Bill Irwin, and asked about their meeting. He seemed to have difficulty placing him. So many people had come through Paris and looked him up. He named some of them: Ruby Cohn, Jack Garfein (who was still there), David Warrilow (on his way to Avignon to do a Pinget play), Sean O'Casey's widow, Eileen (at her behest, Beckett had suggested to Martin Segal that he present the Gate Theatre production of *Juno and the Paycock* in his New York international theatre festival).

We talked about Mike Nichols's projected production of *Godot*. He was dubious; he said he thought of Nichols principally as a film director. Then the nub of his dissatisfaction was revealed. Dustin Hoffman had been in Paris and, though a meeting had been arranged, Hoffman had not come to see him. For Beckett, this was an unpardonable slight. He said, 'He had something better to do.' I spoke again about the reading of *Godot* in Nichols's apartment, how Nichols himself had a gift for comedy. 'Every other line a laugh?' he asked.

I clarified: *Godot* was played, as it should be, as a tragi-comedy. On the other hand, I had seen Rick Cluchey's *Krapp's Last Tape* and been disappointed. He said that perhaps he had been playing it too long, and it was becoming lifeless. Barry McGovern was planning an evening of Beckett's work and wanted to use Jack MacGowran's material, but McGowran's widow wanted to have approval of the show and 'put too many strings on it'. Beckett suggested he do an evening only from the trilogy of novels. In the end, McGovern created his own anthology.

We talked about theatre in London, and he said that he thought the Royal Court had fallen on hard times. But, I said, Caryl Churchill was doing well there, and the company was moving her *Serious Money* to the West End. Beckett seemed to be in a particularly negative mood. One clue to his malaise: he did not smoke and he had only one coffee. Before we left, I asked him if I could take his photograph. Sitting at the table he looked straight into the camera. In the photograph, he seemed to have a contemplative and distant look. As we parted, he said, 'Have a good time in the Dordogne.'

13 July 1988

'How big are they?'

In June 1988, I sent him a letter in advance of a trip to Paris, giving our dates and enclosing a copy of my review of Barry McGovern's evening of Beckett, *I'll Go On*, which which was a high point of Martin Segal's international fes-tival, along with the Gate Theatre's *Juno and the Paycock*.

Again, he sent a picture postcard, of a Paris scene in 1900. He complimented me on my 'impressive' criticism of McGovern's show and said he was also pleased at the news of *Juno*. I noticed that his writing was getting spindlier and more difficult to decipher.

At the request of Andreas Brown, the owner of the Gotham Book Mart, I had brought to Paris three copies of *Beginning to End*, the newly published book of Jack MacGowran's evening of Beckett, illustrated by Edward Gorey. One copy was for Beckett, one for me, and the third for the collection at the University of Texas (which Brown wanted Beckett to sign).

In the morning, Beckett telephoned our hotel, saying he was unable to meet. Somewhat reluctantly, he admitted that he was not well. He had cancelled all his appointments. I said that one reason I wanted to see him was to give him his copy of the MacGowran book and to have him inscribe the others. He apologised for being unable to see me. I said I could bring the books by to his home and leave them. This dialogue followed:

SB: How big are they?

MG: Small. Seven inches by eight inches.

SB: Thick?

MG: Thin.

SB: There is a bin inside the door for packages that are too large for the mailbox. You could put them there.

MG: OK.

SB: When are you leaving?

MG: Saturday.

SB: I will call you in the morning.

After that was settled, we said goodbye. Then the phone rang again. It was Beckett, saying that it would be better if I left the books with his publisher, Jerôme Lindon, whom he planned to see on Friday. 'I will call him,' said Beckett, 'and I will call you back.' Beckett rang back in a few minutes.

SB: I spoke with Lindon, and he will receive you this afternoon. Do you speak French?

MG: No.

SB: Do you have someone who does? My publisher does not speak English. [Long pause, then out of the blue, a moving encomium] I want to thank you for everything you have done for the work in America.

That afternoon I left the books with Lindon. When I arrived in London later that month, the signed copies of *Beginning to End* were waiting for me.

11 March 1989

'I'm the last'

I was in Paris early in March. Beckett phoned me at my hotel. I asked him how he was and he said, disconsolately, 'I'm in a nursing home. I've been in several nursing homes.' I asked if I could come by. He said, 'I'm not much to talk to. But I would like to see you.' He suggested Friday at 5 p.m., then gave me the address. Later in the day he called back and said he had confused his appointments and could I make it on Saturday instead? Yes, of course.

The sign read 'Tiers Temps Orléans. Retraite.' It was a plain institutional building next door to a small hospital on a quiet residential street. I walked through a dayroom in which five elderly people were silently watching television. Finding a nurse, I said I had come to see Mr. Beckett. She led me through a garden to his room, which faced a patio. Because it was March, the landscape was bleak.

The room was small and unadorned, almost as bare as a cell. There were no pictures on the walls, no obvious amenities, only a narrow bed neatly made up, a desk and a table with several books on it, including a dictionary and his schoolboy copy of Dante's *Divine Comedy*, with his notations. In the last year of his life, Beckett was re-reading Dante in Italian. There was a portable television on the floor, on which he continued to watch tennis and football. On the bedside table were a telephone and a diary. There was a wardrobe across the room and what looked like a small refrigerator. His shoes were lined up in a corner. This could have been the setting for a late Beckett play.

Having seen him previously only at the café or walking briskly along the street, it was unsettling to find him in a nursing home. Although the room was warm, he was wearing a tartan dressing gown over his clothes. He was as erect and as alert as ever, but he seemed a stoical, forlorn figure. His attitude could be described as one of embarrassment – not for the Spartan quality of his living quarters, but for his residence there, the fact that he was not well, that he was getting older.

He poured me a glass of Irish whiskey and had one himself. Then he offered me the room's one easy chair and he sat down at his desk. He said that every morning he took a 20-minute walk in a nearby park. His doctor visited him daily, bringing him a copy of his favourite newspaper, La Libération (and an Irish friend sent him a newspaper from Dublin so that he could keep up with rugby results). Meals were delivered on a tray. The food was 'edible', though 'there was too much meat.' While I was there, he smoked a single cigar.

Apologising for his circumstances, and for not being more hospitable, he painted a picture of necessity. Because he had recently fainted, there was an oxygen machine in the room for emergency. But breathing was not his problem, he said. What is? Old age and 'balance'. When he stood up, he seemed somewhat unsteady. His wife was not well, and his doctor was also taking care of her. He said he thought of his life as 'surviving'.

Occasionally visitors had come to see him: Gregory Mosher with the photographer, Brigitte Lacombe; Ruby Cohn was due on Monday.

In New York I had heard Barry McGovern deliver a public reading of *Stirrings Still*, Beckett's most recently published prose piece. I commented that McGovern had instilled it with humour as well as drama. Beckett himself wondered how actors were able to bring prose to life. He admitted there were 'a few laughs' in the piece and then explained the origin of *Stirrings Still*. When Barney Rosset was fired as head of Grove Press, he wrote the first part, then added two more parts, and gave them to Rosset to publish. The book was selling in a limited edition for $1500. Beckett said he had nothing to do with the price. 'Who would buy it?' he wondered. I said that there were probably enough libraries and collectors to take care of the small printing.

In the text, there is a mention of a man named Darly, a doctor Beckett knew during World War II. Asked about him, Beckett said his name was misspelled. It was Darley and he was a friend and fellow worker at an Irish Red Cross hospital in France immediately after the war. He said that Darley was dead and added, mournfully, 'They're all dead,' meaning all his friends from that period of his life. 'I'm the last.'

Using Darley as an opener, I encouraged him to talk about his war days, as a fighter for the French Resistance. Briefly he described how he and Suzannne, his future wife, were in Paris at the time the Germans marched in. They left precipitously for the south of France. For three years, from 1942 to 1945, they lived in Roussillon in the Vaucluse. 'I did odd jobs,' said Beckett. Often he worked for farmers. At the same time, he wrote his novel, *Watt*, the last work he was to write before switching from English to French. One time, Suzanne was arrested by the Gestapo, 'but talked her way out of it'. When I asked if they were on the run, he said, he said, no, mostly they were standing still; they were 'in hiding'.

At the time, he was gathering information for the Resistance. He diminished his efforts by saying, as he had said before, that it was 'Boy Scout work'. But he kept doing it. One reason was because of his fury at the treatment of Jews, who had to 'crawl away', with stars of David affixed to their clothes. After the war, he was decorated with the Croix de Guerre and the Médaille de Résistance. The picture of Beckett as secret agent and hero may seem unlikely but it is accurate. When I credited him with bravery, he attributed it to youth: 'We were young,' he said, as if that explained everything. He of course had the option of returning to Ireland during the war, but preferred to stay and fight in France.

One could trace throughout Beckett's life a full and compassionate commitment on questions of liberty. He was always eager to lend his support to dissidents like Václav Havel and to sign a petition for Salman Rushdie, although he had never met him. It was the principle that counted. He said that he had heard that someone had desecrated a statue of Dante because Dante had assigned Mohammed to a place in Hell. He wondered if censors would go through literary history condemning authors.

I talked about Nichols's production of *Godot* at Lincoln Centre, explaining how Robin Williams and Steve Martin were faithful to the text but diverged in performance. 'You mean he did "business",' he said about Williams. When I described their clownish movements during Lucky's speech, he greeted that with chagrin. I said that Bill Irwin was an extraordinary Lucky and had created a 'sand dance' for his character. He sprinkled sand over sand on the stage set and then danced with abandon on it, a soft shoe sand dance. Beckett smiled at the idea. It reminded him of vaudevillians and silent film clowns of his youth. I said the production brought in a new audience, some of it new to his plays, perhaps new to the theatre. Contrary to other published critical statements released through intermediaries, his conclusion on the production was, 'I suppose it was acceptable.'

What about the *Endgame* at the Comédie Française? He said he objected to it because 'the director was changing things.' He was offended by directors who try to put their stamp on a production. I said that Schneider's strength had been in respecting the text. 'That was a big loss,' he said.

He said he was not working on anything new but had been trying, with difficulty, to translate *Stirrings Still* into French. I asked him if I could bring him anything. He said no, as long as he had his newspapers and his whiskey.

As we talked, he suddenly rose from his chair and began to walk around the room. Was that to keep his blood circulating? 'No,' he said, 'because I'm restless.' As he continued walking back and forth, he began to resemble the character who reaches back into memory in *Footfalls*. It was the final image that I had of Samuel Beckett, pacing out his life, with no end yet in sight.

When I returned to New York, I sent him a letter, commenting on a festival of his radio plays. I asked if they taped the sound of waves on location at Killiney Beach for Barry McGovern's reading of *Embers*. He answered, 'The Killiney beach or "White Rock Strand" is where the girl in *Eh Joe* lay down to drown. Perhaps they had that in mind when recording the sea there.' He added that there was 'little chance I fear' of getting to his country house later in the year. And he closed, 'Glad you enjoyed your brief stay in France. All best to you both. Sam.'

Several weeks later, over lunch in New York, John Calder, his English publisher, talked about his long friendship with Beckett. They had stayed at each other's home. Calder said that Beckett's room in the nursing home was like his house in Ussy: he slept, ate and worked in one room. He recalled earlier days with Beckett in Paris when they would drink and talk past dawn. Sitting in cafés, they would be joined by Giacometti, among others. Calder was with Beckett the day that Hemingway killed himself: Beckett could not stop talking about the suicide, which was something he believed in. The only question was how to do it so as not to inconvenience others.

Calder said that both *Waiting for Godot* and *Mercier and Camier* had come from Beckett's experiences as a courier during World War II: waiting for messages that did not arrive. He thought that the war had changed Beckett's life; it had given him a tragic vision. He said Beckett would have liked his mother to know he was not a failure (which he was, before, at everything) but was less concerned about his father's opinion. This is why he addresses his mother in *Footfalls* and *Rockaby*. During the period when he wrote *Godot* and most of his trilogy, Beckett had a swelling in his cheek, which he thought was cancerous. Although it later turned out to be benign, he believed he was going to die, and he just kept writing. Beckett was still writing, he said – keeping 'a journal of senility'. As he ebbed, he recorded specific details. With his brilliant mind, the journal should be fascinating, Calder said – if it survived him.

In August, Beckett's wife died. I sent him a letter of condolence. He did not respond. In December, I received word that he was sick and was in the hospital. Because the Times had an outdated and insufficient advance obituary, I wrote an entirely new one. Very late on Christmas day, Barney Rossett called to say that Beckett had died, after being in a coma. The obituary was printed on the front page of the Times.

Obituary

'Samuel Beckett Is Dead at 83
His "Godot" Changed Theatre'

Samuel Beckett, a towering figure in drama and fiction who altered the course of contemporary theatre, died in Paris on Friday at the age of 83. He died of respiratory problems in a Paris hospital, where he had been moved from a nursing home. He was buried yesterday at the Montparnasse cemetery after a private funeral.

Explaining the secrecy surrounding his illness, hospitalisation and death, Irène Lindon, representing the author's Paris publisher, Éditions de Minuit, said it was 'what he would have wanted'.

Beckett's plays became the cornerstone of 20th-century theatre beginning with *Waiting for Godot*, which was first produced in 1953. As the play's two tramps wait for a salvation that never comes, they exchange vaudeville routines and metaphysical musings – and comedy rises to tragedy.

An Alternative to Naturalism
Before Beckett there was a naturalistic tradition. After him, scores of playwrights were encouraged to experiment with the underlying meaning of their work as well as with an absurdist style. As the Beckett scholar Ruby Cohn wrote: 'After *Godot*, plots could be minimal; exposition, expendable; characters, contradictory; settings, unlocalised, and dialogue, unpredictable. Blatant farce could jostle tragedy.'

At the same time, his novels, in particular his trilogy, *Molloy*, *Malone Dies* and *The Unnamable*, inspired by James Joyce, move subliminally into the minds of the characters. The novels are among the most experimental and most profound in Western literature.

For his accomplishments in both drama and fiction, the Irish author, who wrote first in English and later in French, received the Nobel Prize in Literature in 1969.

At the root of his art was a philosophy of the deepest yet most courageous pessimism, exploring man's relationship with his God. With Beckett, one searched for hope amid despair and continued living with a kind of stoicism, as illustrated by the final words of his novel, *The Unnamable*: 'You must go on. I can't go on. I'll go on.' Or as he wrote in *Worstward Ho*, one of his later works of fiction: 'Try again. Fail again. Fail better.'

Though his name in the adjectival form, Beckettian, entered the English language as a synonym for bleakness, he was a man of great humour and compassion, in his life as in his work. He was a tragi-comic playwright whose art was consistently instilled with mordant wit. As scholars and critics scrutinised his writing for metaphor and ulterior meaning, he refrained from all analysis or even explanation. As he wrote to his favourite director, Alan Schneider: 'If people want to have headaches among the overtones, let them. And provide their own aspirin.' When Mr. Schneider rashly asked Beckett who Godot was, the playwright answered, 'If I knew, I would have said so in the play.'

His greatest successes were in his middle years, in the 1950's, with *Waiting for Godot* and *Endgame*, and with his trilogy of novels. It was suggested that for an artist of his stature, he had a relatively small body of work – but only if one measures size by number of words. Distilling art to its essence, he produced scores of eloquent plays and stories, many of those in his later years not strictly defined as full length. But in terms of the intensity of the imagery, plays like *Not I*, *Footfalls* and *Rockaby* were complete visions.

He wrote six novels, four long plays and dozens of shorter ones, volumes of stories and narrative fragments, some of which were short novels. He wrote poetry and essays on the arts, including an essay about Marcel Proust (one of his particular favourites), radio and television plays, and prose pieces he called residua and disjecta.

In his 80's, he became an icon of survival. Even as he vowed that he had nothing more to say, he continued to be tormented and sustained by midnight thoughts and nightmarish images. Having discovered what was for him the non-meaning of life and its brevity (man is, he observed in *Waiting for Godot*, 'born astride the grave'), he never stopped looking for ways to express himself. Once in writing about painting, he said, 'There is nothing to express, nothing from which to express, no power to express, no desire to express, together with the obligation to express.' For him that obligation was ineluctable.

From an Outrage to a Classic

Despite his artistic reputation, his ascension was slow and for many years discouraging. He laboured in his own darkness and disillusionment, the equivalent of one of the isolated metaphorical worlds inhabited by his characters. When his work began to be published and produced, he was plagued by philistinism, especially with *Waiting for Godot*, which puzzled and outraged many theatregoers and critics, some of whom regarded it as a travesty if not a hoax.

From the first he had his ardent supporters, who included, notably, Jean Anouilh, the bellwether of French theatrical tradition. He greeted *Godot* at its premiere in Paris as 'a masterpiece that will cause despair for men in general and for playwrights in particular'. In both respects, Anouilh proved prescient.

Today *Godot* is generally accepted as a cornerstone of modern theatre. It is performed worldwide in schools and prisons as well as on public stages and, in its Grove Press edition, is a perennial bestseller. With *Godot* and his other plays, Beckett influenced countless playwrights who followed him, including Edward Albee, Harold Pinter, Tom Stoppard and David Mamet.

The name *Godot*, along with that of the author, is part of international mythology. Godot, who may or may not be a saviour, never arrives, but man keeps waiting for his possible arrival. Waiting, in Beckett's sense, is not a vacuum but an alternate activity that can be as visceral – or as mindless – as one makes it. For Beckett himself, waiting became a way of living – waiting for inspiration, recognition, understanding or death.

For more than 50 years the writer lived in his adopted city of Paris, for much of that time in a working-class district in Montparnasse – a move that was to have the greatest effect on his life. Though he wrote most of his work in French, he remained definably Irish in his voice, manner and humour. Even in his final years, when he lived in a nursing home in Paris, he joined friends in a sip of Irish whiskey, which seemed to warm his bones and open him to greater conviviality. Throughout his life he was as craggy and as erect as a Giacometti sculpture. When he was healthy, he took long, loping walks on Paris streets.

In no way could he ever be considered an optimist. In an often repeated story, on a glorious sunny day he walked jauntily through a London park with an old friend and exuded a feeling of joy. The friend said it was the kind of day that made one glad to be alive. Beckett responded, 'I wouldn't go that far.'

A Star in Studies and Sports

Samuel Barclay Beckett was born in Foxrock, a suburb of Dublin, on Good Friday, April 13, 1906 (that date is sometimes disputed; it is said that on his birth certificate the date is May 13). His father, William Beckett Jr., was a surveyor. His mother, Mary Roe Beckett (known as May), was a nurse before her marriage. Samuel and his older brother, Frank, were brought up as Protestants. They went to Earlsfort House School in Dublin. Samuel Beckett then continued his education at Portora Royal School in Enniskillen, County Fermanagh, and at Trinity College, Dublin, where he majored in French and Italian. At school he excelled both in his studies and in sports, playing cricket and rugby. He received his Bachelor of Arts degree in 1927 and his Master of Arts degree in 1931.

In the intervening time, he spent two years in Paris in an exchange programme, lecturing on English at the École Normale Supérieure. In Paris, he met James Joyce and other members of the literary and artistic set. He was not, as is commonly thought, Joyce's secretary, but he became a close friend and aide, reading to him when Joyce's eyes began to fail. Beckett's first published work was an essay on Joyce that appeared in the collection *Our Exagmination Round His Factification for Incamination of Work in Progress*, the work in progress being Joyce's *Finnegans Wake*. His first poem, 'Whoroscope,' was printed in 1930, followed one year by his essay on Proust.

Returning to Ireland, he taught Romance languages at Trinity. He thought briefly about remaining in the academic profession but decided otherwise. He resigned abruptly in 1932 and left Ireland, returning only for annual visits to his mother. (His father died in 1933, his mother in 1950.) He wandered from England to France to Germany before moving to Paris permanently in 1937. By that time he had published *More Pricks Than Kicks,* a collection of short stories; *Echo's Bones*, a volume of poetry, and *Murphy*, his first novel. Written in English, as were all his works at the time, *Murphy* was about an Irishman in London who tries to remove himself gradually from the visible world.

Settling down in Paris, Beckett became a familiar figure at Left Bank cafés, continuing his alliance with Joyce while also becoming friends with artists like Marcel Duchamp (with whom he played chess) and Alberto Giacometti. At this time he became involved with Peggy Guggenheim, who nick-named him Oblomov after the title character in the Ivan Goncharov novel, a man who Miss Guggenheim said was so overcome by apathy that he 'finally did not even have the willpower to get out of bed'.

In 1938, while walking with friends on a Paris street, he was stabbed with a knife by a panhandler. He was immediately taken to a hospital. One of his lungs was perforated and the knife narrowly missed his heart. Beckett fully recovered from the wound but it left psychological scars. After he recovered, he visited his assailant in prison and asked him the reason for the assault. The man replied, 'Je ne sais pas, monsieur.' More than ever, Beckett became aware of the randomness of life. Before the episode, he had met a young piano student named Suzanne Deschevaux-Dumesnil. She did not rescue him from the knifing – as was sometimes thought – but she did visit him in the hospital. They began a lifelong relationship and were married in Folkestone, England, in 1961.

Hero of the Resistance

With her, he chose to remain in France during World War II rather than return to the safety of Ireland. Both became active in the French Resistance. Forced to flee Paris, the couple went to Roussillon in the south of France. While working as a farm labourer and running messages for the Resistance, Beckett wrote the novel *Watt*. It was often said that his experiences in hiding during the war were an inspiration for *Waiting for Godot* and for the novel *Mercier and Camier*. At the end of the war he worked at the Irish Red Cross field hospital in St.-Lô. For his heroic services he was later awarded the Croix de Guerre and the Médaille de Résistance.

After *Watt*, he began writing in French, which allowed him, as the Joyce biographer Richard Ellmann observed, 'a private liberation from the English tradition.' The five years starting in 1947 were his most intense creative period, producing most of his major work. That year he wrote his first play, *Eleutheria*, and began the novel *Molloy*. They were followed by *Waiting for Godot*, which he wrote in longhand in a composition book. It took him four months. In a little more than a year, he had finished his greatest play as well as the first two parts of his trilogy of novels (*Molloy* and *Malone Dies*).

The Three Openings of 'Godot'

Though he found a publisher for the trilogy (Jerome Lindon at Éditions de Minuit, who remained his French publisher for the rest of his life), the plays were more difficult to place.

Miss Deschevaux-Dumesnil took them from producer to producer, a thankless route that the playwright once compared to giving the plays to a concierge. Then Roger Blin, the French actor and director, agreed to present one. He chose *Godot* over *Eleutheria* partly because it had fewer characters. At Beckett's behest, *Eleutheria* was never produced in his lifetime. It was only when *Waiting for Godot* was in rehearsal, with Beckett in attendance, that Blin fully realised the excitement of his discovery.

En Attendant Godot, as the play was titled, opened on 5 January 1953, at the Théâtre de Babylone, and beginning a lifetime practice, the author did not attend. The first review, written by Sylvain Zégel in La Libération, said Beckett was 'one of today's best playwrights', a fact that was not universally acknowledged. The first London production, using the playwright's English translation and directed by Peter Hall, received generally dismissive daily reviews. It was rescued by Harold Hobson, then the drama critic of the Sunday Times in London, who said the play might 'securely lodge in a corner of your mind as long as you live'.

In January 1956, Michael Myerberg opened the first United States production at the Coconut Grove Playhouse in Miami, with Bert Lahr and Tom Ewell cast in the leading roles as those Beckett tramps, Estragon and Vladimir. Expecting a Bert Lahr comedy, the audience was mystified. As Lahr said, doing *Godot* in Miami was like dancing *Giselle* at Roseland. With both the director Alan Schneider and Mr. Ewell replaced, the play moved to Broadway in April. With the exception of Eric Bentley and a few others, the critics were confounded. Several were abusive. Despite the producer's vainglorious advertising campaign to draw intellectuals into the theatre, the play closed after 59 performances.

What 'Godot' Wrought

That *Waiting for Godot* became a contemporary classic can be attributed to the enthusiasm of its champions and to the profundity of the work itself, which became more apparent with subsequent productions. *Godot* came to be regarded not only as a clown comedy with tragic dimensions but as a play about man coping with the nature of his existence in a world that appeared to be hurtling toward a self-induced apocalypse.

Before *Godot* was produced in London, Beckett completed a second play, *Fin de Partie*, or *Endgame*, as the title was translated. In this dramatic equivalent of chess, Hamm the master oppresses Clov the servant in a bunker looking out on the void of the world. *Endgame* was followed by the radio play *All That Fall* and by the monodrama *Krapp's Last Tape*, written for the actor Patrick Magee. In 1961 after he and Miss Deschevaux-Dumesnil were married, he finished *Happy Days*, about a long and not always happy marriage, in which a woman eventually is buried up to her neck in earth. In 1964 he made his only trip to the United States for the filming of *Film*, the short Beckett movie that Mr. Schneider made with Buster Keaton. Uncomfortable in the hot July weather in New York, he was eager to return to Paris.

About the same time, he wrote a number of stage, television and radio plays, including *Play* (in which three characters are encased in urns), *Cascando* and *Eh Joe*, as well as the narrative fragment *Imagination Dead Imagine*.

In 1969 he was awarded the Nobel Prize in literature for a body of work that 'has transformed the destitution of man into his exaltation'. Karl Ragnar Gierow, secretary of the Swedish Academy, said his writing 'rises like a Miserere from all mankind, its muffled minor key sounding liberation to the oppressed and comfort to those in need'. He was on holiday in Tunisia at the time of the Nobel announcement and in characteristic fashion offered no public statement and refused to attend the ceremony. He sent his publisher in his stead. Reportedly he gave his prize money of $72,800 to needy artists.

As undeterred by the acclaim as he had been by his years of obscurity, he continued to write and to maintain his privacy. His plays and prose became shorter and even terser, as in *Not I*, in which the play's principal character is a woman's heavily lipsticked mouth; *That Time*, in which a spotlight shines on a man's head and his corona of white hair, and *Rockaby*, in which an old woman rocks herself to death. In these plays he chose to deal with what he called 'the battle of the soliloquy', sifting the past and enduring the continuum of life. Two of his prose pieces, *Company* and *Worstward Ho*, were published as short novels. On occasion, he would visit London to supervise a production or Germany, where he frequently worked on television plays and where he staged a definitive German-language version of *Waiting for Godot*.

During Beckett's lifetime he had many close collaborations with actors (Jack MacGowran, Patrick Magee, Billie Whitelaw, David Warrilow) and with several directors, especially Mr. Schneider, who staged most of the American premieres of his plays. When Mr. Schneider was killed in a London traffic accident in 1984, it was a blow to the playwright.

In the same year, the New York Drama Critics Circle awarded him a special citation in recognition of his body of work and in particular for two evenings of Beckett short plays produced that season in New York. One of those plays was *Catastrophe*, written for Václav Havel. It was for Beckett a rare political work about the interrogation of a dissident.

In Beckett's later years, directors staged his radio plays or adapted his prose to the stage. Mabou Mines offered dramatisations of *The Lost Ones*, *Mercier and Camier* and *Company*. Though Beckett was liberal about allowing adaptations of his prose, he was scrupulous in demanding absolute fidelity to the stage directions as well as to the dialogue in his plays. In 1985, JoAnne Akalaitis, a director with Mabou Mines, changed the setting of *Endgame* from a bare interior to an abandoned subway station. Through representatives, Beckett issued a formal complaint against the production at the American Repertory Theatre in Cambridge, Mass., and his objection appeared in the play's programme.

A Life 'Devoid of Interest'
On his 80th birthday in 1986, Beckett was celebrated in several cities. In Paris there was a citywide festival of plays

and symposiums, and in New York there was a week of panels and lectures analysing his art.

As usual, he kept his silence, as in the characteristic note he sent to those who approached him about writing his biography. He said that his life was 'devoid of interest'.

He steadfastly maintained his routine through his later years. He lived on the Boulevard St. Jacques in an apartment adjoining that of his wife and overlooking the exercise yard of the Santé prison. Regularly he visited his country house, some 60 miles outside Paris. He made daily trips to a neighbourhood café where he met friends, had a double espresso and smoked several thin dark cigars. Periodically he wrote brief plays and small prose pieces.

Around him and without his encouragement, his reputation grew unbounded. The Mike Nichols revival of *Waiting for Godot* at Lincoln Centre in 1988 was an event of magnitude, drawing together the diverse talents of Steve Martin, Robin Williams and Bill Irwin and selling out for its entire engagement. This year there was a festival of Beckett radio plays on National Public Radio, reminding his audience that this was still another form that he had mastered.

About a year ago, after falling in his apartment, he moved to a nearby nursing home, where he continued to receive visitors. He lived his last year in a small, barely furnished room. He had a television set on which he continued to watch major tennis and soccer events, and several books, including his boyhood copy of Dante's *Divine Comedy* in Italian.

On July 17 this year, his wife died and he left the nursing home to attend the funeral. Late this year, after he became ill, he was moved to a hospital. There are no immediate survivors.

His last work to be printed in his lifetime was *Stirrings Still*, a short prose piece published in a limited edition on his 83rd birthday. In it, a character who resembles the author sits alone in a cell-like room until he sees his double appear – and then disappear. Accompanied by 'time and grief and self so-called', he finds himself 'stirring still' to the end.

Several days after Beckett died, I spoke to a number of his friends and admirers. Even as they acknowledged his enduring legacy, several wondered if the death of the playwright would lead to the liberation or to the distortion of his work.

When Harold Pinter learned that Beckett had died, he said he remembered their first meeting, in Paris in 1961: 'We literally stayed up all night. We drank all night, from which I never recovered.' Speaking from his home in London, he said, 'He was an inspiration to all writers and certainly was to me. One of the best things ir my life was our friendship. He was a man of immense grace as a friend and as a writer. He didn't admit to any frontiers in his writing. He was fearless in his life and his art.'

Tom Stoppard said, 'What remains the most vibrant memory is the first time I saw a Beckett play, in my case, *Waiting for Godot*. I sat there wide-eyed and, I suppose, with my mouth open, astonished by this piece of magic whereby a complete full-length play with depth and texture and story was constructed out of very much smaller pieces than I ever imagined. I'd always been stretching to do as much as possible in a play. It was a tremendous lesson, his gift of doing so much with such little effort, using small moments to great effect, using a minimalistic landscape rather than a melodramatic landscape. He reached all the highs and lows of much grander drama, and he did it in an extraordinary meticulous way. When I read his novels, I realised he was one of the great humorists of the century. He had the reputation of being a great recluse, but he was so open handed, a recluse with innumerable friends and acquaintances.'

Bill Irwin, who had played Lucky in the Mike Nichols production of *Waiting for Godot*, said that because of its mystery *Godot* was 'a play that will haunt me for the rest of my life. I want to do it again and again.' He remembered his meeting with Beckett in Paris: 'With great trepidation, I said, 'Might I ask a question?' He said: 'Oh. Ask anything.'' This did not necessarily mean that answers would follow. Irwin steeled himself and asked him if he was working on anything – and immediately regretted the question. Beckett suddenly had a 'pained expression' on his face. It was, he said, 'like asking Martha Graham if she were taking a dance class'.

Tom Bishop, a Beckett scholar and close friend, predicted that the plays would now be more available for interpretation and would 'be strong enough to support all that'. He offered his favourite Beckett anecdote, about the pet dog he and his wife had named Beckett. They were too embarrassed to tell the author, but he found out through a mutual friend. Mrs. Bishop asked him if he was offended. Beckett said, 'If the dog doesn't mind, I don't mind.'

Gregory Mosher, who had produced and directed Beckett plays, said, 'He was the first one in theatre to realise that the party is over and to write sublime works about that fact. Courage in the face of pessimism, that's all that's left – and he said that in the 1950's when other people were saying, "Let's build another housing development." ' He recalled the time they were both at the Riverside Studios. A theatregoer approached the author and said, with enthusiasm, 'I've been reading you for my whole life.' Beckett answered, with characteristic drollness, 'You must be very tired.'

Irene Worth said she hoped that with Beckett's death, there would not be a drive to 'free his work' to interpretation. 'That's like trying to free Shakespeare. Great writers are free. All you have to find is how to get inside the work and the mind of the writer.' Speaking about her own affection for Beckett, she said, 'What a solitary man he was to the public and how he enriched the theatre and the lives of people he touched. His extreme modesty sprang from a revulsion with what is considered success, or hype.' She paused and said, 'I always thought he looked like an eagle.'

She said that after hearing about his death, she re-read *Happy Days*. 'It meant so much to me. The joy and the jauntiness of it. It was like a double violin sonata.' One of her most convivial memories was of having a glass of Guinness with him in a pub by the side of the Thames, where they had gone during a break from rehearsals of *Endgame*. She had been watching him direct, and at one point she climbed into one of the dustbins. After trying to explain his stage directions to the actors, he acted them out himself with great deliberation, and in so doing offered 'one of the funniest' performances she had ever seen. 'If only people could have seen the joy in him – and the jokes,' she said. Taking out a copy of his prose piece, *Enough*, she read aloud one of her favourite, most Beckettian passages: 'What do I know about man's destiny. I could tell you more about radishes.'

March of 1990 was a celebratory month for Beckett, first at a conference about the work of Alan Schneider at the University of Wisconsin in Madison, and, the next day, at a Beckett conference at Carnegie-Mellon University in Pittsburgh. Each city was filled with Beckett experts. In Madison, Billie Whitelaw performed *Rockaby*, and then talked about the author. I spoke at both conferences. In a most unusual request, I had been invited to read my obituary of Beckett aloud at the Carnegie-Mellon meeting, which I did before an audience of Beckett scholars and guests. I felt as if I were delivering the longest eulogy.

The following year I was in Paris, for the first time a Paris without Beckett. I visited Arrabal, who spoke about their friendship, which began in 1957 when Beckett wrote a recommendation for him for a Ford Foundation grant. Through this programme, Arrabal and five other European writers, including Günter Grass, Robert Pinget and Italo Calvino, travelled through America. Describing his journey, Arrabal drew a map of the country. In 1967, Arrabal was imprisoned in Madrid for supposed acts of treason. Beckett sent a letter of support, which was instrumental in bringing about Arrabal's release. In appreciation, Arrabal reproduced Beckett's letter on the back cover of one of his collection of plays. Arrabal partly returned the favour when he sent a letter of protest about the recent Comédie Française production of *Endgame*, which, he said, was 'terrible, in pink and with bad music'. Other letters followed, and the production was removed from the stage, for which Beckett thanked him. Arrabal said that for years Beckett had addressed him formally as *vous*; after Arrabal's protest about *Endgame*, he began using the familiar.

Arrabal's obsession continues to be chess. He said he would give anything to be a grandmaster. But, I said, you are already a grandmaster of theatre. It's not the same thing, he said. Then we agreed: Beckett was the grandmaster of theatre. I asked him if he ever played chess with Beckett. With a smile, he said he had not because 'I didn't want to lose to Beckett.'

Conversations about Beckett

Billie Whitelaw, 7 February 1984

'A terrible inner scream, like falling backwards into hell'

A long with Jack MacGowran, Patrick Magee and David Warrilow, Billie Whitelaw became one of Beckett's foremost interpreters. Her kinship with the theatre of Beckett was irrevocably linked with the playwright himself, who for many years was her guide and mentor. Because they worked hand in hand, their relationship may have been the closest of all those between the playwright and an actor. In 1995, she was to write movingly about their collaboration in her autobiography. Eleven years earlier, when she was about to make her first extended New York stage appearance in an evening of three brief Beckett pieces, Rockaby, Footfalls and a reading of the narrative fragment, Enough, at the newly named Samuel Beckett Theatre, we met for breakfast at the Algonquin Hotel. She brought along her scripts of Not I, Footfalls and Rockaby, on which she had written notes to herself, circling words, indicating pauses and characterising the emotional content of the dialogue. Carefully she indicated inflections. Next to the word 'Mother' in Footfalls, she had written 'bong-bong', to suggest that the word, as spoken, had no stress. We talked about the work that had become the obsession of her acting life.

When she teaches a class or gives a demonstration in acting, it is in stark contrast to Ian McKellen's evening of Acting Shakespeare. One assumes that she deals with such consequential minutiae as the quarter-pause, acting while blindfolded and acting only with one's eyes, synchronising the rhythm of a rocking chair with one's own voice on tape;

83

and she would discuss the dramatic power of stasis in performance.

While acting Beckett, she has been confined in an earthenware jug (next to Robert Stephens and Rosemary Harris in Play, *her Beckett début for the National Theatre); been buried up to her neck in earth (in* Happy Days*), and ritualistically paced back and forth across the stage in the half-light (in* Footfalls*). In* Not I, *only her flaming red lips were visible to the audience. At the same time, she has had to reveal her most private emotions, issuing both silent and verbalised screams of anguish.*

BW: *Not I* is a raging babbling mouth. I said that when I die it's going to be buried at my feet.

MG: Martin Esslin was so offended by the colour version of *Not I* that was made for television that he called it an obscenity.

BW: I know what he means. In fact, the words that Beckett keeps on using when he's directing is 'less colour, less colour'. He means less emotional colour. He found the colour of that film too obtrusive. My mouth was bright red, and my lips and gums.

MG: In the Pennebaker film about *Rockaby*, you say you don't think about meaning, you just do the words. It must be difficult to get such shadings among the words. You look at the text and . . .

BW: It's gobbledygook.

MG: Some things are in italics and there are spaces for pauses, but there is no indication about how to deliver the words. How do you find the specific emotion?

BW: Well, I've never done a piece of Beckett's without him.

MG: And if he's not there, you call him on the telephone?

BW: We've rehearsed on the telephone. Once I've got from him an indication of the basic things, how fast, how slow, I go away and I read it and I read it and I read it. I suppose it's a bit like painting. It starts to take on a life of its own. My main job is to keep out of the way of the life that it starts to have. I must have read *Rockaby* God knows how many times, and having done it quite a few times now, I can hear it in my head. I can hear him saying it. I imagine Sam saying it.

MG: Would he read a play to you before you would do it?

BW: Yes. Or we would read it together.

MG: Is your performance the same as your reading with him?

BW: No. A lot of people think he's a dictator, who insists, 'You must say it this way.' He's not. He has a very definite idea of how he wants it to go, but within that, I can emotionally take off on my own. In *Footfalls*, he said, 'I want you to say these two words very quietly.' I said, 'O.K., let's see how quietly I can say them.' And in fact when I did it, I didn't make any sound at all. I just mouthed the words, and it was quite effective. I usually take what he says, and then take it a little bit further. He's always frightened of his things being too emotional. When he says, 'Take all emotion out of it. No colour, no colour,' I think what he means is 'no acting'.

MG: But *Not I* is filled with emotion. It's a frenzy.

BW: He kept on saying, 'Flat, no emotion, no colour, flat,' and I would say, 'Yes, yes.' I think what we finally got back to is something not acted; it just happens. With *Not I* what happened for me was a terrible inner scream, like falling backward into hell. It was the scream I never made when my son was desperately ill. When I first read it on my own, it was about an hour before I could pick up the phone and talk to Anthony Page, my director, and say, yes, I would love to do this – if Glenda Jackson isn't going to do it.

MG: Do you often think about yourself and your own life when playing a role?

BW: Always.

MG: What about *Rockaby?*

BW: I used to sit and watch my mother. [As she spoke, she began to rock in her chair] I'm rocking already. For about five years before my mother died, she had Parkinson's Syndrome. She died just before we did *Rockaby*. She would sit with a blank staring face, hour after hour. I would think, oh God in heaven, what's going on inside your mind? When I do *Rockaby*, I have a picture in my mind, of not necessarily my mother, of someone just sitting and staring out a window at a skyscraper block. How awful it must be to sit at a window, waiting. Perhaps there may be one other person out there. [Her hands begin to flutter]. How awful it must be to sit there waiting for death.

MG: In the film, as you're rehearsing, your hands begin to flutter.

BW: I do that all the time. It's become a sort of joke with Beckett and myself. We both sit there conducting each other. I won't do it on stage, but my feet will be doing it, or my toes. I'm doing it now. In *Footfalls*, there's a weight and a rhythm that I can only get if I'm allowed to conduct myself for a little while. Every single photograph of Sam and myself, we're both doing this [she flutters her hands]. I don't know who's conducting who.

MG: Most of the Beckett pieces that you've done, he's directed you first.

BW: I've never been without him. I don't know what I would do without him. When he dies, I think that's it. I don't know how I would start without him.

MG: *Play* was your first collaboration.

BW: I just got the feeling of that intuitively, instinctively. Before we started rehearsing *Not I*, I had the feeling of that awful scream. With *Footfalls*, I went across to Paris and said,

86

'Help. I don't know where to start.' He read it for me once, and I said that's all I need. Then I went back to London. It didn't end up like that, but I just wanted an indication. Then he came over and we rehearsed. When I was doing *Footfalls*, I felt like a walking talking Edvard Munch painting. Jocelyn Herbert made me this incredible dress: masses and masses of net curtain over a taffeta base, which she bleached out and then dyed. The dress looks like a sculpture, as if it's made out of stone. There's a picture of it in a book about 25 years of the Royal Court. It's Sam's favourite photograph. The Royal Court threw the dress away. I wish to God I'd bought it.

MG: Has Beckett ever seen you do *Rockaby*?

BW: Yes, when we did it at the National, but he won't see anything in front of an audience. It's an emotional thing, fear of fleeing, of putting his head in his hands and shouting, 'Oh Lord, oh Lord,' two words he uses more than any other.

MG: How did the production of *Play* come about?

BW: A friend of mine, Brenda Bruce, had done this funny thing buried up to her waist in arid earth. Then another friend, Patrick Magee, seemed to do a lot of this man's work. I'm not a great theatregoer, so I had never seen any of it. I was at the National Theatre. They said before you do *The Dutch Courtesan*, would you like to do this play by Samuel Beckett? I read it and though I hadn't the vaguest idea what it was about, some strange vibration came off the page. I found it absolute hell to get to grips with, but the actual meaning of it didn't worry me.

MG: But when you do plays by other authors, you understand why your characters behave as they do. Something different must go on when you're playing Beckett.

BW: Yes it does. It's much purer. It's a bit like music. A piece of Schubert either has some emotional impact or it doesn't. *Not I* had the most extraordinary emotional impact when people saw it. I've done two seasons of it, and I will never do it again. I think I would lose my sanity if I did it again.

MG: Your sanity is not in danger with *Footfalls* and *Rockaby?*

BW: No. Sanity's all right. It's keeping that pace.

MG: Is memory a problem?

BW: Oh, yes! With *Not I*, I was beginning to have grave doubts that I ever would learn it. A week before we opened, I said I wanted a cue thing, but it didn't work. Then I said, 'Get me a dwarf with a grand torch and big cue cards.' I'm blindfolded. I couldn't move my head, but I thought if I had a little slit in the blindfold, I could look down at the dwarf. I tried it once with the stage manager, but I just lost speed. I tried to find a way out. I'm not a masochist. It was a bit like driving a racing car. Whenever the car changes gear, the sounds are different. I would go into different musical gears.

MG: With *Footfalls* and *Rockaby*, you have to deal with other sounds, the rocking of the chair, the recorded voice.

BW [she picked up her script of *Rockaby*]: Most of these I've written down: I put 'reaching out to other lonely creatures', 'solitary', 'lullaby'. I think of it as a lullaby. 'Soft, monotonous, no colour, soothing, rhythmic', and 'strongest drive toward death'.

MG: What does 'red' mean?

BW: Red means I've got to repeat it. [She tried to read her writing.] Is that 'quicker' or 'quieter?'

MG: What do those crosses mean?

BW: That's where she starts to cross and I thought perhaps the eyes should open. Obviously I changed my mind and extended the time. Sometimes I find it physically impossible to keep my eyes open as long as that. My eyeballs start to water. I've got very weak eyes. 'To see, be seen.' I think I say 'no' quite sharply, and if I do it makes a startling picture. 'But harmless/ no harm in her/ found dead one day.' I'm asleep in the chair and suddenly the eyes swing open. Don't ask me why. If I was allowed to move, I would be reaching out. I can only do it with my eyes, as with all things, the minimum.

MG: It says 'hurray' on the script. Getting near the end?

BW: That means, from there on I can just shut my eyes. 'Fading.' 'Death?' I've just written my own thoughts: now sinking and fading into death. I didn't know whether she was dead or not. If any university student got hold of these stage directions, I don't know what on earth he would make of them. 'Quick sink down plug hole'. That means something to me.

MG: You're drowning?

BW: No. I'll demonstrate it to you. [She spoke the line in a whisper as if her voice were running in a circle down a drainpipe.]

MG: That's your verbalisation of a visual image?

BW: Yes. I think in pictures. I've never asked Sam what a play means, or what a character is supposed to be doing. But when we did *Footfalls*, I asked him one thing: 'Am I dead?' He thought for quite a long time and then said, 'Well, let's say, you're not . . . quite . . . there.' I knew exactly what he meant and did not ask another question.

This has to do with my niece. She committed suicide the first week of rehearsal. She was found tangled and tattered 10 days later, impaled on barbed wire. It was awful. Sam is very concerned with families. He told me this story of attending a lecture of Jung's. Jung brought in this young girl, of about 21, the same age as my niece. He said, 'The trouble with this girl is that she was never properly born.' I think perhaps Amy, May in the play was not properly born. That's all I needed to know. [At the top of her manuscript of *Footfalls* were written the words, 'She was never really born.']

MG: What other questions have you asked him?

BW: About slower, longer pauses. I've got pauses in here which are marked quarter pauses, half pauses. The first note he ever gave me when we did *Play*, he came into the dressing room and he pored over this script, which is full of one word, dot dot, two words, dot dot, and he said, 'Billie, would you make these three dots two dots,' and he took a pencil and crossed out a dot. That's a quarter pause.

MG: Does it really make a difference?

BW: Oh, yes. I'll read it to you. If I just said, 'Would you like me to inject you again?' that has a different feeling from 'Would you like me to inject you..again.' A little pause makes it more interesting.

MG: How does he feel about actors?

BW: He drives actors nuts. He keeps saying he's been thrown out of more theatres. It can be very trying sometimes. *Happy Days* is a quite a long piece and I spent months learning it, every two dots and three dots, every 'oh well' and 'ah well', every 'ah yes' and 'oh yes', and then he started to rewrite it as we went along.

MG: Do you always keep a jar of your mother's Ponds cream in your dressing room? [When her mother died, she kept the jar as a memory]

BW: It's with me now.

MG: Haven't you finished it? Is it an endless supply?

BW: It's bottomless. I just do that every night. [She touched an imaginary jar].

MG: Were you close to your mother?

BW: She used to drive me mad. I'm sure I drove her mad, but in fact I loved her very dearly. My mother always wanted to act. We came from a background where to be an actress was so totally out of the realm of reality. I couldn't afford to go to drama school, so I got a job in rep being assistant stage manager and general dogsbody. Joan Littlewood became my surrogate mother for a while. She wanted me to join her workshop, but I was under-age. I didn't go back to Joan until I was about 25. But she was one of the biggest influences theatrically in my life. I sort of hedge-hopped. I was trying to get rid of a North Country accent, and suddenly there was a whole wave of what became known as the kitchen sink. I suddenly found that far from actors going around talking as I do now, all the cultured voices vanished overnight. I thought, what the hell's going on, I'm trying to get rid of my accent, and all of a sudden I became employable. Overnight I was dubbed the female Albert Finney, and kitchen-sink-wise I never looked back. It was John Dexter who said, 'Laurence Olivier wants to see you.' The first thing I did at the National was Beckett.

I don't know how to use my voice. I've not been trained. No one's told me how to move. It's going down endless blind alleys. I'm sure I've done my voice and my body irreparable harm. I know I do certain things that a trained actor would say, 'Sorry I'm not going to do that.' When I was doing *Footfalls*, I tore a muscle in the side of my neck. [She stood up and stooped her head, demonstrating the difficult position she had to assume on stage]. Try standing like that for 20 minutes, and I guarantee you'll pass out. The last time I worked at the Royal Court, I passed out, just for seconds.

MG: What was the last time you spoke to Beckett?

BW: About a week ago. We chatted for a long time. He doesn't want me to do *Enough*, because he doesn't like his prose being read on stage. I said, 'Please let me do it.' Very sweetly, he said, 'All right, go on.' I didn't realise we were renaming the theatre, the Samuel Beckett Theatre. I said, 'I'll tell you what I'll do, I'll go on stage with a bottle of Jamesons in one hand and a bottle of Guinness in the other. I'll put them down on the podium when I read *Enough*. Will that make you feel better?' He said, 'Don't take them on and leave them there unopened. Drink the things, for God's sake, drink them.'

MG: Is there a difference between playing Beckett and playing other playwrights?

BW: The actual process is exactly the same for me whether it is Sophocles, Euripides, Beckett or Shakespeare. Once I've found the core, I've just got to put my foot through a fourth emotional wall. Whenever I work with Beckett, I feel as if I'm being blasted off into outer space.

Mike Nichols, 10 November 1988

'You can look at "Godot" and say that it is just another day in Manhattan'

Mike Nichols's *all-star production of* Waiting for Godot *(starring Robin Williams, Steve Martin, F. Murray Abraham and Bill Irwin) at Lincoln Centre, proved to be enormously controversial and popular. It quickly sold out its entire brief run (a projected move to a larger stage never came about). The controversy surrounded the divergences from the text and the perambulations of the performers, in particular Williams. At many performances, Beckett scholars were in the audience, searching critically for alterations. During one performance, one such scholar held a copy of the play in his hand, as if it were a score for an opera or a symphony, comparing the words in the text with those spoken on stage. Momentarily looking up from his book, he realised that Meryl Streep, also in the audience that night, was staring at him, perhaps wondering why he was not looking at the actors.*

In August 1987, in preparation for the production, Nichols met with Beckett in Paris, along with Gregory Mosher, then head of Lincoln Centre Theatre, Walter D. Asmus, Beckett's German director, and Tom Bishop, the chairman of the Centre for French Civilisation and Culture at New York University and a close friend of Beckett's. Soon after the opening in New York, Nichols and I met. He began talking about his encounter with the author, and, point by point, he defended the variations in his production.

MN: Part of the tone of the production came from the surprise of meeting Beckett. The big surprise was that someone can be in a kind of permanent despair and also have such warmth and humour. I thought about that and about the fact that by now everybody knows that Godot isn't coming. It isn't even a possibility. What puts that in relief is that Gogo and Didi are much like ourselves. They're not having such a bad time, but that doesn't negate the basic despair. I think what Pozzo says before his last exit is the most terrible, terrifying sentence in the English language: 'Astride of a grave, the light gleams an instant, then it's night once more.' Beckett put into words what we already know.

MG: Did you talk with him about specifics of production?

MN: He said that as far as the text was concerned, what existed in the various texts was available to us. He said he had made some cuts, and because he knew more about the playing of the play than anyone, I thought we would probably be well advised to make the same cuts, such as the slightly longish section of Pozzo puffing on his pipe, and a few other small cuts, like Gogo and Didi's guesses as to what Lucky calls his dance: 'the hard stool' and something else. Then of course there were the two new lines, three really if you include 'Napa Crappa' instead of Macon and Cacon [a change made for the English language version of the German production, presented at the Brooklyn Academy of Music in 1978]. It's his; he wrote that. Two come from the San Quentin production, for which Beckett wrote Pozzo's lines, 'None of my business.' 'Where do you go from here?' says Didi, and Pozzo says, 'None of my business.' [Initially, Pozzo had said, 'On.'] The other new line, of course, is 'on the Steinway', which I'm also pretty sure he wrote for the San Quentin production and it was in the most recent London production. 'What about your half-hunter? [his watch],' says Gogo. Pozzo always said, 'I must have left it at the manor.' Now he adds, 'on the Steinway'. It's a good laugh and it's certainly the first brand name in Beckett.

These are the only textual changes except for what I think of as a kind of cadenza, when they object vociferously. Beckett doesn't provide any lines. It's where I let the boys ad-lib for about a minute during Lucky's speech. I made a cut. I took the liberty partly because Beckett said, 'If you find anything difficult, you can slim it down.' He offered that, and when Gogo and Didi are examining Lucky, I cut, 'Look at the slaver.'

MG: I've heard that the text in your production can vary from night to night.

MN: It's not true.

MG: During Lucky's speech, Williams refers to Lucky as 'a liberal', applying the word in the pejorative sense used by George Bush in his presidential campaign.

MN: It is a word that Pozzo has applied to himself a minute earlier, when Pozzo says 'I will suffer no doubt but I am liberal. It's my nature.' And then he says, 'What would you have him do . . . dance?' It's a word he applies to himself.

MG: And that's part of what you consider to be the allowed ad-libs?

MN: Yes. How many leaves did you see on the tree?

MG: One.

MN: There are five leaves, but they're in a cluster. We took the more optimistic view. Beckett says four or five. Tony Walton [who designed the show] and I realised that when a tree like that brings forth leaves, they come out of a bud that has several. So they're all at the end of a branch. But they're very distinct separate five leaves.

MG: There's a line in the production about the Academy Awards.

MN: 'I want to thank the Academy.' That's an out and out wild ad-lib of Robin's, and it comes and goes. I think he says that some nights and not other nights. He asked me if that was all right, and I said, 'Yes. I thought it was just all right.' We're very careful and respectful of the text. All the changes are documented. There are certain things we know about *Godot*. Why not explore some new aspects of it? That's one of the reasons we revive plays. I've been very careful about everything Beckett specifies. A road, a tree.

MG: Does he specify a spare tyre, a skull, a bone?

MN: He doesn't because his *Godot* isn't placed in America. Mine is. There is no point for American actors to put on English accents or do all the staging that Roger Blin did in Paris. Why?

MG: Did you tell Beckett that you were going to set the play in the American west?

MN: I told Walter Asmus during that meeting that I wanted to put it in Las Vegas. At the time I was even thinking of having some vague rosy glow on the horizon for the Las Vegas signs. But I also wanted it to be blasted, as though after some great disaster. Asmus said he thought that was a perfect idea for putting it in America and was going to tell Beckett about it. I discussed all this. I wasn't trying to put anything over on anyone.

MG: If it were specifically an American setting rather than generically an American setting, it might have disturbed Beckett.

MN: With Tony Walton and Jennifer Tipton [the lighting designer on the show], as with designers on my movies, I ask for something and they will do it. Then they will leave things out if they don't agree with them, to see if I say anything. In this case, they left out the glow of the signs, and I looked at it and thought it was right that it shouldn't be there. What we have is just enough. What we attempted to do was to express Beckett's ideas for acting by Americans.

MG: I've seen American actors do the play as if they are in limbo.

MN: The limbo is taken care of by the events of the play. No one ever comes down that road.

MG: But what about the tyre, the bone, the skull?

MN: The purpose of those items was to include some American bones in the wasteland, from Georgia O'Keefe all the way through to dead automobiles. I believe that the events we created were Beckett's intention but aren't always expressed, such as when Didi and Gogo lift each other to see who's heavier, Didi waiting and waiting and looking as though he had a watch but long ago lost his last one. These are physical expressions of what's happening. In *Hamlet*, the line, 'take this from this if this be otherwise' is absolutely meaningless unless you point to your head and your body on the first two this's.

MG: On opening night, Barney Rosset was sitting in a front row and had a portfolio of photographs in his lap. Williams took the portfolio and played with it as part of the show.

MN: There is that kind of freedom.

MG: How would Beckett feel about the recognition of the presence of the audience?

MN: It's in his text. Three times he refers to the audience. That bog is in the text. When Didi goes up to the sun, he says, 'Imbecile, there's no way out there.' He looks at the audience and says, 'There's not a soul in sight!' Gogo runs towards the audience and recoils. Didi looks and says, 'You won't? Well I can understand that!'

It's truly a great play, but you can't achieve all of it. Several weeks ago, I wrote Beckett that it was strangely fulfilling not to be able to achieve all of it. No one dares to question Sam. So they question me.

There are certain changes that Beckett made. For instance, Atlas is not the son of Jupiter. He's the son of somebody with

97

a truly peculiar name, which Beckett found out afterward to his embarrassment and changed, but it doesn't sound as good as Jupiter. So he said that those kinds of things are free choice.

MG: What about performance additions, such as throwing sand on sand?

MN: That happens to be a glorious idea, and very Beckettian. As I say, these are physical expressions of Beckett's play. When Ingmar Bergman has Eilert Lovberg's arm up Hedda Gabler's skirt to the shoulder when they're looking at photographs and at last Hedda says, for reasons we can understand, 'Don't, they'll see us,' he's just done that line better than anyone ever has in any production of *Hedda Gabler*. Does that change the text? It's achieving the text. You could argue fruitlessly whether or not that's what Ibsen had in mind. He wrote, 'Don't, they'll see us.' For generations, we've been bored to death while they look through a photo album and Hedda says cryptically, 'Don't, they'll see us.' Bergman achieves that physically. That's our job, that's the director's job.

MG: What about Didi and Gogo's comments during Lucky's speech?

MN: We've scrupulously observed Beckett's stage directions for Lucky's speech, although I would like to hear the speech a little more in the semi-final section. Beckett wants pandemonium. [The stage direction is 'general outcry'. Recalling their meeting with Beckett, Mosher remembers the following exchange: Nichols: What did you mean by 'general outcry?' Beckett: I meant general outcry. Nichols: With laughter? Beckett: Preferably.]

I don't think anybody has achieved the aftermath of the speech as well as we have, the horror of ignoring Lucky. That's always presented as abstract, but it isn't abstract. It's about cruelty. That cruelty is physically expressed in this production. Didi is pissed off at Pozzo. He is outraged. That's between the words.

MG: At various points, Robin Williams mimics voices from Hollywood mythology.

MN: Didi says, 'Will you not play with me?' Gogo says, 'Play at what?' The whole next section is play. There's no reason why part of their play can't be references to things in our culture. The idea is to have fun when you're playing. One of the most masterful things in the text is the juxtaposition of humour and horror, perfectly expressed in Gogo's pants falling down at the most heartbreaking tragic moment. Godot isn't coming. We're born astride a grave. Down in the hole, lingering, the gravedigger puts on the forceps, we have time to grow old, the air is full of our cries, habit is a great deadener. Thirty seconds after that, Gogo's pants fall down. That's what Beckett wrote: the juxtaposition of comic bits and the yawning of eternity.

MG: What is your view of Lucky?

MN: I saw him as a former writer intellectual who becomes a Dav-El [limousine] driver who wears a Grateful Dead T-shirt under his uniform.

For Pozzo, we just thought about all kinds of stars and tycoons, people of humble origin who achieve wealth and renown and build towers in New York. You can look at *Godot* and say it is just another day in Manhattan. Sometimes homeless people are quite well dressed but they have no socks and their feet are dirty. These people who sit on benches in traffic are not terribly different from Gogo and Didi.

MG: They just took a wrong turn and ended up in Las Vegas?

MN: They certainly worked in one of the lounges there long ago.

Deborah Warner, March 1994

'I am no cowboy when it comes to text'

After the death of Beckett, the reinterpreters and the deconstructionists were ready to move, while Edward Beckett and Jérôme Lindon, as executors, stood firmly on guard, trying to protect the legacy and the memory of the author. In March 1994, there was a major collision, as Beckett's Footfalls, a 20-minute monodrama, suddenly became the centre of a theatrical tempest. The play deals with the death in life of a woman who has devoted herself to her aged mother. Ritualistically, the daughter paces back and forth on a narrow strip of floor, with the space and the action carefully prescribed by the playwright. A haunting interior dialogue, it was created for Billie Whitelaw, who first performed it under the playwright's direction at the Royal Court Theatre in 1976.

In 1994, Deborah Warner, one of the most adventurous of young British directors, presented the play at the Garrick Theatre, with Fiona Shaw reinventing the role of the protagonist. In this version, the actress went 'walkabout,' moving from the stage to a promontory on the edge of the dress circle and then back to the stage again. In both locations, she postured and grimaced the character's pain. The performance disregarded the author's designations of costume, lighting and stage directions, and the supposedly disembodied voice of the character's mother (Susan Engel) seemed to come live and clear from the orchestra.

Seeing the production at its first performance, Edward Beckett thought, in the manner of a Beckett character, 'This can't go on.' Five lines of dialogue had been transposed from mother to daughter. At the insistence of the Beckett estate, the

*lines were returned to their original speaker. But there were
other problems. 'The production destroyed the play's timing,
atmosphere, the ghostly aspect,' Edward Beckett said. 'The
hypnotic effect of the words was shattered by the peram-
bulation. And for what purpose?'*

*He was particularly disturbed because the play was un-
familiar to many in the audience: 'When Deborah Warner
does Shakespeare or* Hedda Gabler, *people know it and can
evaluate it against what they know. In this case, they can't.'
Speaking as a professional musician, he added, 'Every piece
of Mozart can be played differently, but everyone has to play
the same notes.' Asked what would qualify as fair interpretation, he pointed to the Mike Nichols revival of* Waiting for
Godot *at Lincoln Centre. 'A genuine attempt was made to do
the play,' he said.*

*'I don't want to preserve the plays in aspic. I think that
would be harmful to Sam and to the estate. We're not trying
to produce cloned productions, but we insist they play the
play as Sam wrote it. This was the first high profile contre-
temps. I don't know what happens in village halls: 50 people
seeing a Beckett play in Burnham on Crouch. But you've got
to make a stand. You can't abandon Sam to the wolves.' In
response, the Beckett estate ended the production after the
one week London engagement and cancelled the European
part of the planned tour.*

*Billie Whitelaw had also seen the performance. Reached at
her home in Sudbury, she said she was depressed by it.*

BW: I felt as if Samuel Beckett were burned at the stake.
I felt numb, physically ill. If this extraordinary piece of
experimental theatre can be so appallingly misunderstood by
two very talented people, it doesn't hold out much hope.
I listened to Fiona being interviewed on Kaleidoscope. The
interviewer said it was marvellous how she opened up the
play, putting it in two different venues. It's only my opinion,
but *Footfalls* was a turning point in Beckett's work. All arts
are contained in this one piece. It was like being painted with

light. He used me as a piece of sculpture. I told him you could hang it on the wall.

The character is not rushing around the house. She is trapped within the room. It's written in four movements, the same thing with *Rockaby*. The movements get less and less. I walked so slowly, Sam said to me he felt that I disappeared into fuller's earth. Fiona played it as a brain-damaged spastic, walking upstairs and downstairs in my lady's chamber. When I did it, it was like a cobweb or smoke, gradually evaporating. The play had a magical, mystical, almost religious quality. [She recalled Beckett's advice to her and imitated his voice.] 'Inward, Billie, always look inward.' There was nothing inward about that performance.

Deborah Warner and I spoke soon after the opening, and she still seemed to be in a state of shock.

DW: It was a rather astonishing over-reaction. We had planned to play one week, to explore the possibility of looking at the late plays to see whether or not the individual ones could be presented in their own right. They're always packaged in double, triple or quadruple bills. *Not I* was another piece I considered. These plays are only suited to each other by virtue of having been written by the same dramatist. It's too high-level protein to reel from *Not I* to *Footfalls*. It was a big experiment. People were invited to go to the West End at 9:30 for 20 minutes. The whole thing was eclipsed by the banning. I'm pretty shaken by having a piece in infancy stopped forever.

MG: Why did you choose to do the piece the way you did it?

DW: Beckett is clearly a great 20th-century writer, and the piece is by its very nature experimental in form. He was exploring the parameters of theatre. I chose the Garrick Theatre [which was then dark, i.e. no other show was running there] purposely because I wanted a certain atmosphere of restriction, the pained imprisonment of that mother-daughter relationship and the wider imprisonment of that house: a devastatingly lonely place. I wanted the metaphor of an empty dark house and a dark theatre, in which the daughter would be crushed between the floor of the dress circle and the roof of the theatre, between heaven and hell.

MG: Were you aware of the prior productions of the play, beginning with Billie Whitelaw's version?

DW: I only saw Billie's on television, after we began rehearsals. But I'm aware generationally: those are productions of a certain time. Now the play should be done a little more bravely . . . to release Beckett for a new generation. If there's a Beckett cliché, it's someone standing in a white light in a black box set. In its time, that was highly innovative. But I have to carry with me the history of my time.

MG: What kind of production of *Footfalls* would you object to?

DW: I would find great fault if the text were cut, if there were no attempt at engaging with the emotional heart of the piece. I think it is a greatly emotional play. There have been reckless productions of Beckett, and this is not one of them.

I wish Beckett were here. We would be in dialogue. I don't believe I'm doing damage. I'm responding to why he is a very great artist. I am no cowboy when it comes to text, and neither are Fiona Shaw and Susan Engel. I wouldn't want my production of *Footfalls* to be remembered as a whacking great cause célèbre. Beckett will withstand productions that will delight some and offend others. The estate is reluctant to allow him to take on sure wings of his own.

Martin Segal, 17 October 1995

'You could tell him that we were two bankers'

O*f all Beckett's friendships, one of the more surprising was with Martin Segal, a highly successful American businessman, an actuarial specialist active in creating corporate retirement funds. Segal also has an intense interest in the arts and for several years was head of Lincoln Centre. He was the founder of the First New York International Festival of the Arts. He originally met Beckett in the early 1960's through Henry Wenning, who was both a business associate of Segal's and a primary collector of Beckett manuscripts and papers. Among the many differences between Beckett and Segal was simply the one of size. Segal is a small compact man; Beckett was tall and imposing. Walking down the Boulevard St. Jacques or having a drink in the Ritz Hotel bar, they must have been an odd looking couple. My conversation with Segal took place in his Park Avenue office.*

He provided me with copies of letters to and from Beckett. The letters, from 1965 to 1989, chronicle the growth of their friendship. Along the way, there are personal glimpses. In a letter, written from Malta in 1972, Beckett said, 'We are holding out not too badly and enjoying again the sun and sea on this grand old rock. Among its many pleasant effects is that of making me wonder how I ever wrote a line and if it is conceivable I'll ever write another.' While rehearsing Happy Days *with Billie Whitelaw at the Royal Court in 1979, he proclaimed it as his last job as director and confessed, 'I am a tired and dull old dog these days.' In December of 1980, Segal offered to be the host for a private dinner party in celebration of Beckett's forthcoming 75th birthday.*

Characteristically, Beckett declined: 'I dread this year and shall have to fly from it all.'

MS: There's one letter that I've moved heaven and earth to find that for me was the most valuable letter. I can't find it. I sent him a telegram saying we were coming to Paris and would meet him any time convenient to him. We arrived at the hotel, and there was a note, 'Dear Edith and Marty. Meet me at the PLM Sunday morning at 11. If you are not there, I will know you wanted to be. Love, Sam.' I remember it verbatim. That for me was absolutely what he was like.

MG: When did you first meet him?

MS: I had a colleague, Henry Wenning, who owned 20 per cent of the company. Henry retired in 1958 because he was very interested in first editions. He opened a rare bookshop across the street from Yale. Henry was Irish-American, very handsome and an exceptional person, well spoken and well read. A few years before that he had become the representative of Beckett in this country, selling Beckett's manuscripts. Beckett had been very badly burned by other people. Henry owed him some money for manuscripts he had sold, and he knew I was going to Paris. He asked me whether I would give Beckett the money, knowing that the exchange rate was more favourable for U.S. currency in Paris than it was for French francs in the United States. I took some $2000 with me and exchanged it at the Chase bank in Paris. I called Beckett. He asked me to come to his apartment. I went to see him at 11 o'clock. I rang the bell and handed him this envelope with money that was due him. He said, 'Would you like a drink?' To my amazement, I said, 'Yes.' Four hours later, he and I were still talking and had polished off a bottle of Irish whiskey. We established a rapport. He wanted to know about my background. I told him when I was a kid I had done *papier-mâché* masks. He was very interested in masks at that time.

I was kicked out of high school when I was 16. I was such a poor student. I never went back. I went to work full-time. While I was in high school, I was an art major and wanted to be an artist. Fortunately for the world of art, I didn't become one. But I had a great teacher, who realised I was untalented and steered me in the direction of other things, and one of them was Theatre Arts monthly and stage design and costume design, puppetry. I got very involved in the visual arts as related to theatre, avocationally. Then I didn't do anything formally in the arts until I started the Film Guild of New York at age 22 for foreign films in the United States. A dismal failure. My first real involvement in the arts was when I formed the Film Society of Lincoln Centre in 1968.

MG: When you met Beckett had you seen his plays?

MS: No. I had read *Waiting for Godot* and I knew of him. I was very interested in Joyce at that time and knew a little bit about their relationship. I also knew from Henry Wenning how generous Beckett was in keeping an eye on Joyce's daughter and the family. Henry liked him as a person very much, quite aside from representing him.

MG: What did you talk about for so many hours?

MS: We talked about American theatre. I didn't know enough to speak with great authority about it. He would ask questions. He was really interested in my youth and Henry's youth. He was quite intrigued with the fact that Henry had been a labour organiser and part of the extreme left as an Irish Catholic. I was an immigrant to this country, and he was very interested in how I was educated, or not educated. He asked a lot of questions. I learned enough about him to really love him. He was a lovable person. He asked me to look up a writer named Julius Horwitz. He wanted to give him a gift. That's when I learned how much money Sam was giving to writers, to poets, to others. He never said anything about it. All his life, when he made some money and when he won the Nobel Prize, he used that money for other people, people he never knew. He had never met Julius Horwitz. He had read something that he had written. He asked me to meet him, and I wrote him a letter saying Horwitz looked like a deserving person. He sent him money.

He didn't say much about his war experience, but he did speak in passing about what he had done in the Vaucluse. I think he became ill at that time, that was the beginning of some of his lung problems. He was also very interested in having his plays done in the United States. He said so, point blank, in the very first meeting, but I didn't have the remotest idea how one went about that.

Much later someone asked me how we met, and I didn't feel free to tell him the precise nature of the meeting. Sam said, jocularly, 'You could tell him that we were two bankers dealing with each other.' Which is a joke when you consider that I was delivering some money.

MG: 'Bagman to Beckett' would be the headline.

MS: Neither one of us was accustomed to that kind of encounter.

MG: Did you ever bring other money to him?

MS: No. Only time. It was a very pragmatic reason. Henry was very sensitive to the reason: if we could do better with dollars in France, why shouldn't we do it? It was typical of Henry's thoughtfulness about what was in Sam's best interest.

The meetings we had after that: there was one I considered quite important, when he told me he was coming to the United States to work with Buster Keaton. We tried to arrange things for him, but he didn't want to do anything but meet Keaton, do the film and go home. Maybe he would spend an extra day or two. I talked to him twice during the filming. He adored Keaton's work, but it was a very unhappy experience. He couldn't wait to leave the country. It's clear that that incident discouraged him from coming again. I also think he wasn't comfortable in a really brand new situation. When you think about how long he lived in that apartment, when you think about the small coterie of intimate friends, when you think about his travel: he went to the same places for vacations. I tried endlessly to get him to come again, to arrange for him to be involved in speeches or seminars or meetings. No.

He was very family oriented in an odd way. Our son Paul, who was 17, was going to Paris, and I thought he might enjoy meeting Beckett. I had heard that Beckett was interested in new forms of holography and colour. I wrote Sam a note, and he said he would see Paul. They had a long lunch. Paul described a machine he was making in which colour changed in relation to music. Paul later became an architect. Beckett volunteered to take him to meet Le Corbusier, his good friend. Paul thought that was such an imposition; he said no. He regretted that. But Beckett subsequently gave him a little drawing of Corbusier's as a personal gift.

MG: How often would you see him?

MS: At least every year. We'd meet for coffee mid-morning. He also came to the bar at the Ritz; he liked it, he would survey the scene. He lived very simply, but he didn't mind the exposure to a more luxurious situation, as long as he didn't have to belong to it. He called me to tell me he was getting the Nobel Prize. He was on vacation at the time, and he was already not well. We agreed to meet in Paris, and we had dinner together to celebrate it at the Grand Véfour. By that time, the papers were full of him, so when we came in everybody recognised him. He had scrambled eggs, or something like that.

MG: And champagne?

MS: I think he had a sip. I had champagne.

MG: What did he say about the Nobel Prize?

MS: We sat there for about three and a half hours. The place was riveted to him. It was really an extraordinary experience. You know the French are very convivial about food and wine, and normally in a restaurant you would hear the buzz. But they were so watching him, it was really eerie. He acted like it was nothing. He didn't seem aware of all that. He didn't seem surprised by having won it. He didn't seem unsurprised. It was as if it was just another event in his life. He looked at it that he could be a little freer about money matters. That was the closest he got. That night should have been photographed. When we finished dinner, I volunteered to get him a taxi. He said no, he was going to walk home from the restaurant. A long walk. He was wearing the usual sweater. It was winter time, and he had a shawl thrown the way the Irish know how to throw a shawl around their throat. It was a misty night. He looked frail. He walked into the night. If you wanted to visualise a poetic situation of a great writer going back to wherever he was going: I just stood there, I couldn't move. I thought he's going off alone; that was so evocative of his writing, of his person. And yet he could be as warm and as caring. He always asked after the children and always wanted to know what you were doing.

MG: Did he ever think about going to Oslo for the presentation?

MS: No. He wasn't well. I think he already knew he had cancer at that time. He certainly had a serious lung problem. You know he was never a person for crowds. He didn't function well in crowds. I went to his apartment three or four times but never met his wife. I knew she was there. Henry never met her, and they were very close.

MG: Would he ever talk about the work?

MS: Only in terms of who was working with him. He would express irritation how somebody wouldn't follow the directions and how he was comfortable directing himself when he could. He was basically saying that he didn't want anybody to do anything other than what he had visualised precisely. If you praised something, he would say, 'Oh, well.' We had seen *Not I*, and I complimented him on it. I told him it was absolutely a riveting experience. He loved Billie, you know. He said, 'She suits the work,' as if he had nothing to do with it.

MG: Would you talk about politics, worldly affairs?

MS: Now that you ask the question, I wonder what we talked about. We got together for an hour, two hours. During the McCarthy period, he said something about the country going through difficult passages. He was reluctant to be critical. He would ask about the state of theatre in New York. My theatre knowledge was that of a reasonably informed lay person who was going to the theatre once in a while. We did talk about philanthropy once. He thought that people in the United States were saving money by contributing to non-profit organisations. I pointed out to him that if you make a dollar gift and it's tax deductible, the government is paying 40 or 45 per cent, but if you didn't give it, you would have all of it. He had a hard time getting that into his head. I was already involved with the Film Society at Lincoln Centre, and he was very curious how it got started, and what we were doing. He was very curious what Charlie Chaplin was like, when he came here.

The distinction between the work and the person is that he wasn't a doleful person. He was very warm, very affectionate, very interested in the conversation. The only time I ever saw him angry was when we had a date with him for an afternoon, around 3 o'clock. We had great difficulty getting a taxi. We were due to meet at the bar at the PLM. We were maybe 40 minutes late. I was dying. It was pouring rain. Traffic was terrible. We arrived, and as you know he was meticulous at meeting you on time. He said, 'You're very late.' We were prompt people, and I explained. He wasn't exactly in a forgiving manner for the first 15, 20 minutes of the conversation. It was clear he was very irritated.

MG: He wasn't always cheerful.

MS: No. I don't ever remember him looking cheerful. His face wasn't a cheerful face. It was only when he talked that you realised he wasn't a doleful person. I don't think I remember him ever laughing out loud. He would smile. The only time I ever heard him complain was when he talked about his illness. He would say, 'I'm not up to that anymore.'

Once we had an appointment, and he called to say he really wasn't feeling well. I think that did get him down. I saw him eight months or so before he died, and he was very unhappy about that. We knew him for such a long time when he was ill that the final illness was the logical step at that point.

MG: Would you go to art galleries with him?

MS: He would recommend: did you see, did you hear, did you read? He was interested in what was happening to artists, writers in particular. I had the feeling he had a dozen, maybe two dozen people that he would talk to alone, that he would be comfortable with, for an hour, two hours. Very responsive. If I wrote a note, I would hear from him right away. And courtly, as you know. His manners were easy, just nice. We didn't see each other often, but I really grieved for him. When he died, I had the clear feeling which I have to this day: he was a great man, a great artist and unlike many artists a fine person. If you meet as many artists as you and I have met, you realise that what they produce and what they are personally can be very different, and you're sometimes much better off not knowing who it is that wrote the book or did the play or painted the painting or did the music. I don't feel that way at all about him.

MG: Did knowing him make you understand and appreciate the plays more?

MS: In a curious way, it puzzled me. It made me understand the plays more because he was a laconic person. He was not given to long talking. To that extent, you knew that behind a few words there was emotion and feeling and understanding. In that sense, yes. I can't honestly say that if I hadn't known him I would have found his work as interesting as I did.

MG: Have you had a similar relationship with any other great artist?

MS: Not really. With one or two exceptions, Fred Astaire being one, I was a little chary in not wanting to be disappointed. To this day, I don't hang around with artists. Many

111

artists I'm happy not to meet. I'm happy to hear their work, applaud it, support it, get it funded. Sam was an exception. He was such an exception that I think it's unfair to other relationships which could develop. There's a kind of personal standard. The fact that he was so successful financially in his later years and gave it all to the art, to other writers, is so different from what's going on in the world of successful artists. I know artists who are worth millions and millions of dollars, who don't give you a nickel for anything. When I'm talking publicly and am asked what I think of them, I say they're fragile people, they don't know how long they're going to last. I apologise for them, but privately I have a very dim view of many of them. Sam was different. He didn't want to be encumbered. All you have to do is look at what he wore all the time: that satisfied him.

I think it would have been daring to spend days together, because he was such a private person and so sensitive to the way he was with his friends. I think I would have been worried about how to manage the whole day and evening with a person like that. I think I would feel that I was being intrusive. I was especially concerned about keeping the conversation and the relationship at a level that I thought he was comfortable with. In a way, you were like that, Mel.

MG: Perhaps you could have said, 'Sam, what's bothering you today? Is there something I can do?'

MS: He knew me well enough after a while to know that I would do almost anything if I thought it would make him feel better or happier.

MG: I was curious about the range of people Beckett saw. I know there were a lot of actors.

MS: And artists. I gather he saw a lot of other children of friends. It was his way of being a friend. If he thought it was important enough for you, for your child to meet him, then it was important enough for him to want to do it for you as a friend. I don't know anybody who had a bad word about him.

I think that the artists that worked with him all had enormous regard for him as a person, in addition to his work. And people that he helped swore by him. He considered civility an important part of mankind.

I've got a story to tell you. Fred Allen used to write his own stuff and regularly his executive producer would get hold of him and say, 'Fred, you've got to change this, you've got to change that.' One day, Allen turned to him and said, 'Listen, where were you when the page was blank?'

Edward Beckett, 15 December 1995

'Mackerel and white Beaujolais'

*O*n a cold wintry day I took a train from London to Hemel
Hempstead to see Edward Beckett, who lives with his
wife and their daughters in a cosy suburban house. He is tall
like his uncle, but is more filled out and has a heartier
disposition. A flautist, he is a late-comer to theatre, but was
close to Samuel Beckett and was the natural one to be named
as an executor and protector of the work.

*In the newspapers that morning were reproductions of
Prince Charles's Christmas card, a photograph of the Prince
between his sons who were encased in urns, looking like
characters in Beckett's* Play. *One paper compared the card to*
Endgame, *confusing ashbins with urns, but it certainly was a
Beckettian image. I began by mentioning the picture to
Edward, who, laughingly, said that he had seen it, and it was
'quite extraordinary the way that his work has permeated'
our culture.*

MG: What was it like growing up with Samuel Beckett as
your uncle?

EB: In the early years, he was the uncle who lived abroad and
sent all those nice stamps and occasionally a little present. It
was only in the later years at school that I realised he was
quite somebody. Of course, even at that time, he hadn't
achieved the public exposure that he did later. I was born in
'43, and *Godot* came in '56. When I was 13 or 14, I became
aware of him in another light all together. In the later years I
really had to adjust. It still comes as a bit of a shock that
somebody you've grown up with, your uncle [is Samuel
Beckett]. I went to Paris when I was 19, and we had a

perfectly normal family relationship. During my years in Paris, he looked after me, we went out together, we had meals and played billiards.

MG: For all the mystique surrounding him, he always seemed open and affable.

EB: Absolutely. The only time he really clammed up and became awkward was when someone attempted to make his work a subject of discussion. Otherwise, people from Ireland and university, and actors would see him and he would have a purely human relationship. People who knew his work and had performed his work – he had a special feeling for them. They talked to him about many other things than the work.

MG: We talked a lot about tennis.

EB: Yes. Tennis, cricket, rugby. During all the conversations I had with him over the years, he would discuss his work only occasionally, and it was mainly to do with problems in rehearsals.

MG: But he wouldn't talk about the actual writing; he wouldn't say he had problems writing.

EB: No. Not at all. The nearest he would come to that would be talking about the problems he had in translating his work, looking for little nuts that he had to crack from one language to another. Translating *Comment c'est* into English was a hell of a task. He found it very gruelling. The thought of tackling *Worstward Ho* . . .

As the years go by and as the biography [by James Knowlson] is coming, I'm learning more than I ever knew about my uncle and who he met. He didn't talk about what he was doing or who he was seeing. If he was seeing you there was no cross-referencing between his other friends. He wasn't a chatterbox. Without thinking about it, most people will pass comments on other people, or refer to conversations they had with other people. He would never do that. I think he was quite rightly cautious. Something pops out and it's latched on to and it's disseminated. But that was in his nature . . . He seemed to be able to really get through to the heart of somebody, and see who they were, what they were. He seemed to be able to understand people very quickly.

MG: He indicated to me that he didn't go to performances; he went to rehearsals. Was that true? Did you ever go with him to the theatre?

EB: Not the theatre, but concerts and cinema, but never to a play. I do believe he went to performances, for instance, of Pinget and some other writers.

MG: But not his own plays.

EB: No, although he did attend some performances in London. He used to steer clear of first nights like the plague, but if he were around and not back in Paris, he would come in and see something. I know he saw Billie Whitelaw doing *Not I*. I wasn't there but somebody who was there told me he was sitting in the audience. He was 100 per cent riveted. He was sitting bolt upright and honing in on that incredible performance.

MG: You went to movies with him.

EB: We went to a few Buster Keaton movies. Suzannne went along, on the Champs Élysées. We watched *The General*, which he had seen many times before. We also went to see *The Hustler*, with Paul Newman. He liked that; he was very fond of billiards and pool. He was a great concertgoer. I'm sure in the early days he went to a lot of theatre, but when he got involved himself, it was too near home. Later on, he didn't want the attention, the inevitable media attention that he would have had.

MG: I wondered if the very idea of seeing the plays and hearing his words would make him self-conscious.

EB: That wouldn't have occurred to me. Perhaps he wouldn't have been able to restrain himself from saying, 'No! That's all wrong.' The same reason he seldom went to vernissages unless it was a very close friend. He would wait until the opening party was over and then come in the next day and look at the paintings. And first nights are very unique occasions. They're not like other audiences. Perhaps that's what he objected to; there wasn't a real audience there.

MG: Did you visit him often in Paris?

EB: I lived there for four years, as a student at the Conservatoire. Generally when he was in Paris we had a weekly evening, either all together with Suzanne, or the two of us. If she didn't want to join us, the two of us would go off somewhere and have a meal and a game of billiards.

MG: Did he win?

EB: Yes! Almost always. I could never come to terms with French billiards. There are no pockets. A special technique, working your way down the cushion, just working the balls and getting them into a corner. He was good at that. He used to beat me at billiards and at chess.

MG: And tennis?

EB: I never took him on at tennis, although he would have beaten me at that. I wasn't much of a player. Golf I could hold my own. He was quite fun to see. He had been a jolly good player. The first couple of holes were scrappy. Then he remembered what it was all about.

MG: Would he ever recommend books for you to read?

EB: No. In a very gentle way, he might talk about some book or other. My aunt [Suzanne] would occasionally give me books that she read.

MG: What was she like?

EB: Quiet, very sweet, to me anyway. She was a very strong

personality. She decided what path she was going to take. She wasn't a waverer at all. At the same time, she had very gentle sides with her friends. She was very affectionate.

MG: The picture of her taking *Godot* and *Eleutheria* around to producers shows a real determination.

EB: Absolutely, and when Sam would flag, she would take up the torch, and keep going. She wouldn't accept defeat and let him get depressed about it. He did anyway. She would just go on and do what she thought she had to do.

MG: There were long years when people were not listening.

EB: He was writing and not selling.

MG: When were you living in Paris?

EB: '61 to '65. It was about the time of the first performance of *Happy Days* and *Play*. There was a lot going on, and I was a party to some of it.

MG: How did you feel about those plays as a young man?

EB: They captured my imagination. I saw the plays and accepted them for what they were. I didn't think them particularly outlandish. I must say I wasn't a great playgoer. They came more easily to me. I can't remember being shocked by them, being alarmed or troubled by them, or being bored by them.

MG: I wished that he had talked more about them.

EB: Yes. I sometimes wish also that I had prompted him a bit more or perhaps shown more interest in the writing. But I was so wrapped up in my music at the time.

MG: The question remains whether, if prompted, he would have revealed anything more about the work. Perhaps he was waiting for the right prompting.

EB: I don't think so, because occasionally I did ask him, pushed him in that particular direction, and he would be evasive. He certainly wasn't waiting for me to put the right question. [Laughs.] I don't think that at all. But I'm sure if at that time I knew more about what he had been doing I probably could have got a bit more out of him. Perhaps he would have answered my questions, but you felt he didn't want to, so you didn't ask them. He avoided it.

MG: Occasionally we would talk about the physical writing of the plays. He wouldn't talk about the inspiration.

EB: Yes. The last two years, when we were down in the country, he showed me these books of false starts and 'bad week,' page after page in this exercise book scratched out. Couldn't get it going. He would talk about 'false starts'. Of course now people say there are a few questions one could have asked. As I say, at the time I felt they weren't the questions to ask. He didn't want to answer them. He didn't want to go into detail.

MG: Certainly one would never consider direct questions, like, where did the word Godot come from?

EB: The only clue, probably a red herring, that he gave me, was about the name Hamm. In Paris there are two famous Hamms, the music shop in the rue de Reine and a firm of lift makers. We were in a lift and there it was: Hamm. The academics have shown us that Hamm and Clov are entirely different, so they think. I think Sam himself came clean about those. I'm convinced that Hamm just came to him, thinking about the music shop. Then the other nice connotations made the name more attractive to him. He did make a happy discovery at the end of his life when he was translating *Comment dire*. The last line is 'what is the word', a double meaning. [It is both a statement and a question.] That came straight out of the translation. Then to find it had that ambivalent feel about it. Perhaps the choice of Hamm had that as well. It had more than one connotation. It had an extra attraction to him.

I realise I'm a terrible disappointment to people, hoping that I might be a fount of inside knowledge, but I'm convinced that Sam talked more about his work and things to other people, people in that world, like yourself, than he did to me.

MG: But in the family you were the closest to him.

EB: I suppose so. Yes. His later family. He knew my cousin John well. I was the person who saw most of him, and he really took me under his wing after my father died. I was certainly very fond of him and he seemed to be very fond of me, and we had a good solid relationship. He was very good to me. Knowing what a busy man he was, he must have set aside a lot of time to see me. Knowing the amount of people he had to see. At the time I didn't think of it. Every week he set aside an evening, if he could.

MG: Would he ever bring other people along on those evenings?

EB: No. Occasionally we met up with somebody afterwards. I'd go to the flat, and even if my aunt wasn't going to come out with us, we would all sit around. Sam and I would have a drink, and Suzanne would talk. If the three of us went off, we'd have dinner and then split up. But if it was just the two of us for dinner, we'd often meet up, especially when Con Leventhal [a close friend from Beckett's Dublin days] had come to Paris, or was that after I left? I sometimes blur in the time when I was a student in Paris, and all the years afterwards. We'd meet up with people, perhaps in a bar.

MG: Artists, writers?

EB: We used to see some of them at the Falstaff bar on rue Montparnasse. I can't remember a time when we sat with somebody else for a meal.

MG: He wouldn't invite Ionesco?

EB: No, but occasionally we'd meet him in Montparnasse at a little restaurant called La Palette. Ionesco used to eat there. They'd greet each other, salute each other. That was it. Only one occasion do I remember them actually exchanging a few words. I was under the impression that Sam and Ionesco got on. It wasn't the animosity there seemed to be between him and Sartre. One evening Sartre was in the restaurant. Their salutation was to ignore each other. That was the way of Paris life: you saw people in a restaurant and you didn't accost them. The thing that he loved about Paris was that you could go into a restaurant and have a meal with somebody, and somebody you knew would come in and you wouldn't have your evening broken into. People respected each other's privacy.

MG: When you were with him, would you often meet other people?

EB: I met other writers. I met Pinget, and quite a few theatre people: Matias who did the designs for *Happy Days*, and the actors and actresses, Barrault and Jean Martin. Introductions weren't arranged. Just people he was friendly with, who we met either during productions or just met in the street or in a café. Chance meeting. Musically, he was great friends with Mihalovici. We used to see him.

MG: And he would talk music with you?

EB: Yes, very much so, about musical performances and performers. But there again, I wasn't a composer. Perhaps if I had been interested in composition, we might have talked rather more deeply about music and what it meant.

MG: But he heard you perform?

EB: On quite a few occasions. He steeled himself to come to the final competitions at the end of the year when you got your prize or were sent back for more practice.

MG: Sam played the piano.

EB: He did. He was quite a reasonable performer. He played Haydn, Beethoven, Chopin, some Schubert. I'm not quite sure which was his music and which was Suzanne's music, because she was a professional player.

MG: Would he ever play Gershwin or Cole Porter, or old Irish songs?

EB: No, but he could play by ear quite well, vamp out with accompaniment. There are stories about him getting out on the piano at rowdy parties in London. But not in my presence. I heard him play Haydn pieces. This was down in the country. I never heard him play in Paris. Down in the country where there were no neighbours.

MG: Tell me about the house in the country. It was very removed and private?

EB: We used to drive down when he had the car in Paris. He'd keep it stored in the garage next door. Since demolished. We would drive down in this old 2CV, bumping over the country roads, stop off for lunch somewhere, time it nicely. We'd stop off at a little restaurant, the Cheval Blanc, where they had white Beaujolais, which he was very fond of. It was a very simple house. In fact, my father was an architect and helped design it. It was basically a single-storey rectangle, divided about two thirds along its length, on one side a living room split in two, buttressed by a screen . . . the bedroom and a study, sitting room, bathroom, small kitchen, boiler room and entrance porch. It was built on about half an acre, a triangular plot, with roads running either side of it, country roads, very little traffic.

MG: Did he keep a garden?

EB: As estate agents would say, 'Mainly laid to lawn.' It was all grass and trees. There were no flower beds. He did a lot of his work there. He used to go down there for solitude. I think he felt that Suzanne didn't like it there anymore. She felt isolated. Also, I think she knew that he needed the space. When he was there, he'd do a tremendous amount of walking. He could look over the valley. He used to take a few days to settle in, walk himself in, and then start working. The longest I stayed was for about five days. Occasionally I would come down for a weekend. If he was coming down on Friday, I'd come down with him, and then perhaps go back on the train on Sunday and leave him down there.

MG: Would he cook?

EB: Oh, yes. A dab hand at rice, nice rice, soup and vegetables. Basic, wholesome stuff. No creations. None the worse for that. He would cook but we would always go out to restaurant's in the nearest town, La Ferté. The nearest village was Ussy, but there was nothing there. There might have been a café. He didn't go there much. La Ferté was where the railway station was and where he kept his car when he didn't drive in Paris: his eyesight got too bad, and the crashes too frequent. So he kept the car in a garage there, and he did all his shopping down there.

MG: He gave the house to the farmer?

EB: Yes. When he realised he couldn't go down there any longer. When he went down at first, he rented a room from a local farmer, and they always used to look after the place when he wasn't there: clean it when he was coming. They'd air the place, and the son would cut the grass. When he decided he couldn't go down there, he decided it should go back to the land again, which was very fitting. I think the son is living there at the moment. His family needs the space. The idea was that the parents once they gave up farming, they would retire up to the house and hand the farm over to the son.

MG: Where is the car? It should be in a museum.

EB: Well, it was. It was bought by some Swiss fellow, whose speciality was buying famous cars. The latest one that came up was Mussolini's car. His Lancia had apparently been auctioned. Sam gave his car to the farmer's son, because he liked tinkering around. It was in a bad state of repair, and this fellow appeared on the scene and offered many Swiss francs. They felt a bit awkward about it, so they rang me up and said, do you mind? I said no. They sent me a picture of it. The man went bankrupt; he probably embezzled all his funds to buy these cars. I don't know where it is now, probably a pile of rust somewhere.

MG: It would be an interesting idea to have a touring exhibition of cars: Mussolini's, Sam's . . .

EB: I don't think the 2CV would tour very well. There were two 2CV's that I knew of, in the time. One, when I came first, which was terribly beaten up, and then he bought a slightly more up-market 2CV, slightly being the operative word. It was green, sort of khaki green colour. Irish people have a natural affinity with green. I don't think it was a considered choice, just what the dealer happened to have at the time. The previous one was grey. There's no loyalty to green. They're not like real cars. They're like toys. They're great fun, wonderful to drive.

MG: And he stopped driving because of his eyes.

EB: He still drove from the garage to the house. But he gave up driving in Paris because he had no peripheral vision because of his cataracts. Driving in Paris is absolutely lethal. You need more than peripheral vision. I was very glad he decided to ditch driving in Paris.

MG: Would he ever visit you?

EB: He did. Not to this house. He never came here, but he came up to our previous house near Harrow. I think he was at the Riverside [Studios, in London] with Cluchey and his crowd. I picked him up and drove him out for the evening: mackerel and white Beaujolais.

MG: Would the Becketts ever have large family gatherings?

EB: In Paris we met up with John, my cousin, and his family. The family wasn't that big. Sam's father was one of five brothers, but the family's size diminished after that.

MG: Did you know your grandparents?

EB: I knew my grandmother. My grandfather died 10 years before I was born. I have strong memories of her.

MG: Did Sam ever talk about her?

EB: I think so, but no stunning statement comes to mind. My memories of her are of a quite forbidding woman, but I was young. We went for most Sunday lunchtimes: my father, sister and mother. They were quite formal affairs, but afterwards we would go out on the lawn with her and play clock golf. She had flower pots sunk into the lawn, and she'd come out and play that, and then we'd go inside for a game of Happy Families. That was a card game: Mr. Fish the fishmonger, Mr. Bull the butcher, then you've got to collect the families in your dealt hands. Then you pick one up and put one down and try to collect the four members of the family. She was dressed in black. She never came out of viduity.

MG: A word I'm familiar with.

EB: [Laughs.] As a young chap, I was minding my p's and q's on those Sundays. But looking back, she was quite soft.

MG: She had a great influence on him.

EB: Ah, yes.

MG: Always a mystery: where genius comes from.

EB: There's no history of any writers in the family, as far as anyone knows. There's a musical background. His grand-father's wife was a musician, had music published, song arrangements. His uncles were an interesting bunch. His uncle Gerald, who was John's father, was a GP. He was a very good pianist. He and Sam used to play duets together. His uncle Howard was a very good chess player, and his uncle Jim was an Irish champion swimmer, so they were quite a gifted lot. With Sam, it was a late flowering. He was purely an academic and scholar till he was 22. But there certainly was no literary background in the family.

MG: Did it ever make him happy to create?

EB: From what I can gather: no! [Laughs.] We know his 'inability to express but an obligation to express.' It was a hell of a struggle, but one he had to go through. It wasn't much fun, but there must have been some feeling of relief and satisfaction. I think he sometimes seemed to be happy with things that came out well.

MG: Working with actors must have brought him some pleasure.

EB: Yes, but does any writer have pleasure in the process of writing, of getting it onto the page? I know from being a musician: whenever anything is totally impossible I retire to the music room and take the flute out and play. I know it's something I can relax in and feel that I can do.

MG: What would Sam do in such a circumstance?

EB: He would retire to the piano, and play, I think for solace and for relief.

MG: I would think that reading was a consolation.

EB: He read a tremendous amount. He did continuously read and go back on things he had read previously. Dante was perpetual reading. He also read thrillers. He was fond of Len Deighton. Sherlock Holmes. Mysteries. Conan Doyle. His house in Ussy was full of those. And some of those French thrillers. He would relax with those. I know he read Robert Louis Stevenson extensively.

MG: I half expected that someday someone would write a thriller with Sam as a spy, based on his Resistance days.

EB: It would be a pretty slim book. I always get a shock: there's a television series, *Quantum Leap*, and the hero is named Sam Beckett.

MG: Would he ever talk about his war experiences?

EB: No. He wouldn't talk about that period. It was a painful time, one that he really didn't want to go back into.

MG: At what point did he tell you he was going to make you an executor?

EB: In the last eight months before he died, he asked me if I would help Lindon [his publisher] in looking after things because he realised it was just too much and also that Lindon wasn't an English speaker and would need a bit of help. I said, of course I would do it. I think he said it would be a lot of work. I couldn't imagine what work there would be. It was something I took on readily. Obviously at the beginning, just because of the nature of things there were a lot of things happening. I had to find my feet, find the way things had to be administered and had to be run, and to meet the people. Then there was a quiet period, and then a second phase came along, when people start thinking what can they do. People probably think I spend every day, but I don't. I can keep on with music quite well but I do devote quite a lot of time to correspondence and to seeing people.

MG: Do you have to approve all productions?

EB: No, basically, a lot of the standard productions are approved by the agents. It's understood that stock productions, small theatres around the country, schools, institutions can go by on the nod. There's nothing controversial about those. Obviously when there's something bigger than that, a major tour or a new West End production, then we get involved.

MG: Do you think of yourself as a watchman over the work?

EB: Lindon and I are trying to do what Sam did in his lifetime. Curtis Brown sent over all the requests to him for vetting and he'd just scribble on them, OK, or no, not this one. I just feel I'm to continue that work for him. It's only when you get controversial productions then that starts to become very difficult.

MG: Recently there was a production of *Endgame* Off-Broadway, in which an actress played Clov. Would that have come through you?

EB: There are added complications in that half of the plays were written in French, and would be controlled by Éditions Minuit or the SACD in Paris. If somebody wanted to do a French play in New York, it would be licensed through our agent in New York, Georges Borchardt. If there is any doubt, he would check back with Paris. But if the same thing happened to *Krapp's Last Tape* or *Happy Days*, then the agent would check back with me. The English plays are controlled through Curtis Brown, although obviously with *Godot* and *Endgame* in English we don't have to go to Paris all the time. Quite often you grant a licence to someone to do a play and there's no mention of changing the sex in one of the roles, and sometimes it never actually comes to light. You can't vet every single production. It's only with a larger production, or it's announced that it's going to be done in a certain way, that the estate gets involved in trying to stop it.

MG: Like Deborah Warner's *Footfalls*.

EB: That only came about because I went to see the preview night. She had applied for the rights and the rights had been given but no mention had been made of the fact that it was going to be staged in mid-air, and that lines were going to be slightly doctored. I had a seat in the back and I couldn't understand why the front row seats were blocked out, until suddenly the actress was a foot away, and clinging on to the front of the balcony for dear life. I noticed that some of the lines had been transferred from one actress to the other. So at that point I had to get back to Curtis Brown to say, what's going on? And I had to make the decision of course of whether to let it go or whether to stop it. Obviously I referred back to Lindon, and we decided that was the end [of the production]. It's always a very difficult decision. If you stopped it, the actors would be out on the streets again, and perhaps money would be lost on productions. The compromise was to disown the production publicly, take no royalties from it and make sure it didn't go any further. So we refused permission for it to go to France.

We're not entirely restrictive. We're not, as Deborah Warner said, conservers of museum pieces. Not at all. All sorts of productions and interpretations are possible but still staying within the framework of the piece.

MG: Have there been other such things?

EB: At the Edinburgh Festival there was an all-female *Godot*, with a cigar-smoking Pozzo. One of them was dressed up as Groucho Marx with glasses and cigar. What we object to are people who try to use the work to further their own careers, to project themselves, not seriously attempting to interpret Sam's work, just using it as a convenient wider net to jump on. You can't just draw a clean line anywhere. What's doubly difficult is if you let something go, say we allow an all-female *Godot*, well, that's it for all time. Having let one go, the door is wide open. As you know, Sam gave permissions for very strange things, Mabou Mines productions and adaptations of his prose works. He regretted them. His expression about *The Lost Ones* with David Warrilow: 'Permission was granted for a straight reading. This is a very crooked straight reading to me.' But he had the right, and people respected that right, to say, I really don't want that sort of thing anymore. Sorry, but. Basically, he didn't like transpositions from one medium to another, from reading to the stage.

MG: That's why he didn't want *All That Fall* staged.

EB: Eventually his arm was twisted to authorise *All That Fall* for French television, which he regretted bitterly. A travesty. It should never have been visualised, which I think is the big problem when prose work is visualised in one person's picture of what's in the ears. When a book is adapted to a film and you see a film, it's jolly hard to go back to the book again, and create your own world, the magic of prose text.

MG: Has anyone tried to film any of the novels?

EB: There was a project to film *Murphy* that Sam had more or less given the go-ahead to. To a couple of German film-makers. But it's never happened.

MG: No one's done *All That Fall* on stage again?

EB: It comes up, but as a non-visual staging. Not adapting it for the stage. It's a text that people want to perform.

MG: I remember seeing it at the Public Theatre in New York as a radio play on stage.

EB: The Royal Court is now talking about doing it as a radio play. And the double twist of recording it at the theatre for a radio broadcast. No set, no movement, just voices.

MG: And sound effects.

EB: And sound effects, so it would be like people attending a studio broadcast. Which I think is just about legitimate. Of trying to be flexible and non-restrictive, people wanting to hear this text, and let's face it, you can't expect any radio station to broadcast *All That Fall* once a month, every month. It's a pity to have a text like that unavailable.

MG: People will always want to do it fully on stage, as *Under Milk Wood* is done.

EB: I don't feel any problem saying unequivocally 'no' to that because that's something that Sam tried and hated, didn't want done, this visualisation. The stage adaptation of *Company* was done with his benevolent consent. He was not enthusiastic, but he allowed it to happen, on the condition that there were no projections on screen, but just a person there on a couch.

MG: He was interesting in filming *Film* again.

EB: There have been a few versions. There was a version done by the National Film Theatre many years ago and filmed in colour, without asking anybody of course. I can't say anything against that. That's a script, and it's there to be interpreted. The thing about the *Film* was that it was a bit of a botched job anyway. It was cut down to fit within the budget and time allowed. It wasn't as he conceived it at all. The requests to refilm the television plays, . . . *but the clouds . . . ,*

Ghost Trio, that's a difficult one. Sam's own versions which he worked on carefully with the South German Television people: they exist and are readily available. If a painter has painted a picture and created the visual things that he wanted – should one be allowed to repaint this? We don't feel the need or desire to have these plays refilmed. That's the knotty problem you've got to wrestle with, where you've got to make an artistic judgment and a moral judgment, and away you go.

MG: What about the problem of *Eleutheria*?

EB: [Laughs.] I thought you'd come to that. That's a real knotty one. Or if you just take a direct attitude, there's no problem there at all because Sam didn't want it published. He certainly didn't want it performed. But the fact is that publication was forced upon us, we've had to go against Sam's wishes which he expressed almost to his dying days. There was talk about a Pléiade edition of all his works being produced. He said, 'In theory fine, but not *Eleutheria*.' Put it in some obscure appendix, but that wasn't to be included in the body of work. Well, it's now in print, in French and English, for various reasons. So should we then do a double dirty deal and put it on the stage?

MG: Have you ever heard it read?

EB: No, I haven't heard it.

MG: This is a crucial question.

EB: Absolutely. It is crucial in one way. I have read it myself, obviously, both in French and in the translation that's been published.

MG: But there is a difference between reading it and seeing actors do it.

EB: Yes. The thing is even if I had heard a reading of it, or seen a bootleg production of it, should that affect my decision, or Lindon's decision? He's the custodian of *Eleutheria*.

It's definitely a French work. There's a strong moral problem. No matter how good it is, Sam didn't think it was any bloody good at all.

MG: He could have been wrong.

EB: He could have been wrong, of course. There is that possibility, but it's a knotty one: whether we should take that decision and say, well perhaps he was wrong about this. We will just have to wrestle with that one.

MG: Hearing it read by good actors, I felt it was highly theatrical, though the play needs cutting.

EB: You say that it needs cutting. I think that's something you just couldn't do. Morally, you have no right to cut it, you have no right to tidy it up and make it presentable. The only way is to accept it as it is. All its warts and all. I don't think you can really countenance having it put in order, to make it easier to produce. You just have to accept that that was a play the author didn't consider a success. If it's ever staged, it shouldn't appear in a different form.

MG: Then there are three possibilities: it's never staged, it's staged in its original form, or it's staged in an adaptation. The third is one you would not allow.

EB: I think that would be immoral. The other two? First you have to decide if you go against Sam's wishes. Having done it once, do you compound it by putting it on the stage?

MG: Just as David Warrilow came to him with his idea for *The Lost Ones*, someone might have come to him with an idea about *Eleutheria*. He might have agreed, or said, in the words of Gogo, 'Nothing to be done.'

EB: He was asked many times whether it could be published. He knew damn well once it's put into print you're on a very steep slope indeed, to stop it slipping on to the stage. We're faced now with this predicament, that it's there for people to buy and read, and of course any director worth his salt would be raring to put it on the stage.

MG: Barbara Wright is doing another English translation of it.

EB: She's working on it. Faber has the English rights, and they didn't think much of the American edition. They missed so much. It's not a serious translation.

MG: The RSC is interested in it.

EB: Of course. If it's published, Faber would like to make a bit of a splash. They don't want to publish a play that's not going to be performed. We're not rushing into anything.

MG: If it's going to be done, it should be done by a company like the RSC, at the highest possible level.

EB: Oh, absolutely. If you're going to have this revolting – revolving stage . . . It would take some staging, and it's quite a large cast. Obviously, if it was done, it would want to be done at the highest level, and then people could evaluate it. It would be foolish to close the door and forget about it. But we don't want to precipitate ourselves into doing something. I think there's a natural reluctance to do the dirty on Sam twice, in quick succession.

MG: What else is happening with the estate?

EB: We're trying to get a few productions in London to coincide with next year as an anniversary year, his 90th. BBC are putting on some things. They have this film to show, which I'm awaiting with some trepidation because yours truly appears in it. And there's the Lincoln Centre festival. I'm trying to document all the music, the settings of Beckett. A lot of them are not published. Mihalovici wanted Sam to provide a libretto for an opera. Sam said he couldn't, so they did an operatic *Krapp*. It lasts maybe 50 minutes. He actually worked with him and went to hear it. It was put on in Germany and in Paris. He thought it was reasonably success-ful. It's a big part for a baritone, Krapp.

My life could be spent going around to every symposium and production, of course. It could be open-ended. I could go into the production side myself and encourage people, but

I don't think that's called for. I do what I can to act as a cata-lyst and as a guardian, and try to equate those two things in as reasonable a way as possible. My greatest help is that Lindon is there. He knew Sam and knew his thoughts. Without him, life would be an awful lot more difficult.

MG: One regret is that there weren't recordings made of Sam's voice. Are there any?

EB: Of his voice? Very few. I know some people have recordings on their answering machines, and they're holding on to them. There is one recording I know of, of him doing a reading, but that's in private hands. I wish that when he did his coaching sessions of Lucky's speech that that had been recorded.

MG: Or that Billie had a private tape recording.

EB: Or that I had. You couldn't. There were just things you couldn't do. I could never even ask him to sign a book. Things you couldn't bring yourself to do, because you knew he'd say yes.

MG: I asked him to sign a photograph I took of him. He signed his name on his turtleneck.

EB: I'm glad you did. I think I felt so protective of him.

MG: Are there any other unpublished works?

EB: No, there's nothing left. A lot of fragments that are all in Reading [where there is a Beckett Archive in the University]. He emptied out his trunk. I'm afraid there are no unpublished plays. There are some small texts, a lot of small poems that remain unpublished. Scribbled on beer mats and pieces of tablecloth. They're also down in Reading.

MG: You're not thinking of bringing out a book?

EB: No. Reading [University] themselves might: bring out bits and pieces. But there are no other major works to come out, I'm afraid.

MG: Do you have a lot of his work here?

EB: Manuscripts? No. I have virtually all he's published in multiple copies in every language under the sun. But there are no manuscripts. They're all in universities.

MG: As I remember, *Godot* was one of the last ones he held onto.

EB: Oh, yes. That's still in Paris. That's still with us.

MG: You still have his Paris apartment?

EB: Yes. I kept that on. I use it, but not often enough, to my chagrin. I love to be over there. I was over there for three weeks in April, working with the Sinfonietta.

MG: Does the place still exude a feeling of Sam?

EB: Very much so. Very much so. In the early years. Of course, we've repainted it and recarpeted it. The early few years after he died, there was this awful thing: his presence. I expected to have him appear at any moment, he and Suzanne. Because I had spent so much time in the place with both of them, I could hardly sleep there. I kept imagining these spectres, voices; it was so strong. If I had been that sort of persuasion that you could conjure up people, that would be the place to do it. It hadn't been touched since they moved in in the early 60's. We had to do something, but even with freshly painted walls and newish carpets (but nothing too garish), his presence is very strong. His study is of course exactly the same, with the books exactly the same, they're all there, all his books, his desk. Nothing has been changed.

MG: And you're not going to open it as a museum.

EB: Certainly not. He didn't leave his pen on the desk. The telephone is still there on the desk. A certain number of the paintings are still on the walls. I'll never change that. I can't imagine stripping that all out, and all the books won't be moved.

MG: Balzac's house and Victor Hugo's house are open to tourists.

EB: Open to tourists. If perhaps he hadn't given Ussy away . . . but the flat is small and utilitarian in a 60's block in Paris. If people traipsed up the stairs, all the neighbours would take extreme objection to that.

MG: It will stay as it is?

EB: I think so. Not as any sort of mausoleum, but because I like it like that.

Selected Reviews
and Essays

24 October 1969

Enigmatic, Nihilistic, Brilliant: Beckett is Expressing – What?

A Nobel Prize Appraisal

VLADIMIR: Well? Shall we go?

ESTRAGON: Yes, let's go.
They do not move.
Curtain.

The last moment of Samuel Beckett's masterpiece, *Waiting for Godot*, with all it says of the continuing futility of mankind, perhaps comes close to summing up the nihilistic vision of the elusive, enigmatic, incontestably brilliant author. Life, says Beckett, is unendurable, but it is endured.

Oddly, almost any extract from Beckett contains the essence of Beckett. He is consistent to his flinty core. Even his pauses are idiosyncratic. His style is a poetic mixture of statement, re-statement, omen, resonance, and, mostly, silence. He deprecates words, ennobles silence. 'Every word,' he has said, 'is like an unnecessary stain on silence and nothingness.'

Purposely, he has immobilised his characters. Although in *Godot* they gambolled a bit as they waited, in *Endgame* he puts Nagg and Nell in ashcans. In *Krapp's Last Tape*, Krapp conducts a dialogue with the droning sound of his voice on a tape recorder. In *Happy Days*, Winnie is up to her waist in earth – and sinking. In *Play*, three people are encased in urns, with a spotlight striking their faces when they speak.

By strict measurement, Beckett has a small body of theatrical work (although considerably amplified by his six novels, and his short stories, poems, radio and film scripts and his critical essay on Proust). Only *Godot*, *Endgame* and *Happy Days* are generally produced unsupported by companion pieces. But who is to say that the haunting *Play* is not a full-length play, even though it lasts only 12 minutes?

To a Broadway audience, if he ever were to be produced there again, Beckett would probably seem stupefyingly untheatrical, but in a true sense he is one of the most theatrical playwrights since Shakespeare (and taking a cue from Jan Kott, Peter Brook showed their inter-relevance in his *Endgame*-like production of *King Lear*). Properly done, his works are not only profoundly serious, but also profanely funny, with tramps and clowns, self-mocking ironies, and with an absurd comedy that sometimes even verges on vaudeville.

Sadly, at least in the United States, he is perhaps more written and talked about than seen. It is generally agreed that *Godot* was his first popular success. It exposed him to the world, and caused a re-examination of his novels (which have the same theme as his plays – the search for meaning and the discovery only of meaninglessness).

In the years since, *Godot* has been discovered away from the commercial theatre – by students, scholars and regional theatres. It is now a generally accepted classic, probably the cornerstone play of the modern theatre. The United States, for one, has caught up to *Godot*. The truth is that, in it, Beckett reflected what was to become a general malaise, a confusion and desperation about the future of man.

Although some of Beckett's work, to the uninitiated, may seem prolix, actually all of it is spare – as lean and as hardboned as his own cadaverous frame. Each word is carefully chosen. Beckett is the consummate artist, undeterred by sentiment, popular fashion, politics, theatrical rules of order or literary influences. Beckett is singular.

He is not only the most influential living writer for the theatre, he is the seminal figure in modern drama, and such later playwrights as Edward Albee and Harold Pinter freely acknowledge their admiration – and their debt to him. Even before *Godot* was produced here on the stage, Pinter said of him, 'He is the most courageous, remorseless writer. He brings forth a body of beauty.'

Beauty? Some may say, as they contemplate Beckett's bleak landscape, not beauty, but aridity, failure, aloneness, impotence. But there is a beauty of a strange kind. As Martin Esslin has written, if an artist in despair, such as Beckett, finds 'that at the core of existence there is nothing, then the very act of saying so contains the artist's and the world's redemption.'

20 November 1970

Jack MacGowran in
the Works of Samuel Beckett

J ack MacGowran in the Works of Samuel Beckett is the quintessence of Samuel Beckett offered by the quintessential Beckett actor, Jack MacGowran. The evening is pure and perfect.

The one-man show, produced by Joseph Papp, opened last night at the New York Shakespeare Festival's Newman Theatre, a splendid setting. For people who know Beckett the show will be an absolute pleasure; for those who do not, it will be something of a revelation.

Author and actor are so commonly rooted in spirit that if Beckett were an actor he would be MacGowran, if MacGowran were a writer he would be Beckett. It is an exact meeting of actor and role such as one seldom finds in a play, and almost never finds in a one-man show. This is not just a reading, or an impersonation, but an incarnation of the work and of the man.

The stage is set starkly – one rock, subtle swirls painted on the floor evoking the circular, timeless quality of the world of Beckett. Into the circle walks Jack MacGowran. Robed in a long, stained great-coat, ankles bare, shoes loosely bound, head shaved to stubble, face sepulchre-grey, eyes red-rimmed, MacGowran is a tramp, a Beckett tramp, not a clown, but a man reduced by life and forced to go on living.

MacGowran is the Beckett man – aware of the meaninglessness of existence and the necessity to exist, desperately longing for death but unable to die, facing again and again the inevitability that life is merely a stop – a long, seemingly endless stop – between birth and death.

142

Beckett has always been suspicious of words. They can never convey enough, but they are the solitary conveyor. Like the Beckett man forced to endure against his will, Beckett as poet is forced to use words. The theatre, which he came to in middle age, gave him a freedom and a new dimension. Wordlessness could be performed. Beckett's plays, beautiful on the printed page, exist to be acted (and I would like to see every one of them acted by MacGowran). One of the many surprises in an evening of surprises is that Beckett's prose and his poetry exist to be spoken.

One is amazed to hear Jack MacGowran bring Beckett's difficult novels to life. With effortlessness, exactitude and understanding, he transmits them – in an eloquent Irish voice (which reminds one not only that Beckett has a marvellous flow of language but also that he is very Irish).

Listen to MacGowran tell Molloy's story about the sucking stones, the 16 stones he deposits in his four pockets, hoping not to suck the same one twice in succession. After endless hilarious circumlocutions, finally finding the perfect path through his pockets for the stones, MacGowran confesses, insightfully, 'Deep down it was all the same to me whether I sucked a different stone each time or always the same stone, until the end of time. For they all tasted exactly the same.' And so, apparently, does life to Beckett.

Listen to him speak a passage from the novel *Watt*, in which Beckett is both in love with and deeply offended by nature – for the redundancy and futility of the seasons: ' . . . and then the whole bloody business starting all over again.'

For this extraordinary show, MacGowran has selected, with Beckett's 'advice and approval', words, phrases and passages from the novels, poems and plays, including *Waiting for Godot*, *Endgame* and *Krapp's Last Tape*. In *Krapp*, he has found, of all things, a love scene, which he recounts with caressing tenderness. With few exceptions – such as Lucky's apocalyptic speech from *Godot* – the selections are not set pieces. What MacGowran has done is to weave a tapestry of Beckett.

143

It is clearer than it has ever been that the man is the work, that Beckett is extremely subjective, his work all interrelated and completely consistent – which is not to say repetitious. He can say almost the same thing in quite different ways.

He can be merrily self-deprecatory ('An old foetus, that's what I am'), fiendishly ironic ('I regret nothing. All I regret is having been born'), mournfully solemn ('The end is in the beginning and yet you go on'). And MacGowran has precisely the right shading for each passage. Finally he is heartbreaking as he recites the last lines of *The Unnamable*. Stooped in agony, he wails, 'I can't go on,' then slowly begins to stand erect, and continues, without pause, 'You must go on, you can't go on, I'll go on.' Helplessly, man begins the cycle again.

'There I am,' MacGowran concludes at the end, and we agree. 'That's enough, that's enough,' he appends, and we disagree. One could spend many more than two hours seeing, hearing, experiencing *Jack MacGowran in the Works of Beckett*. It is an evening in the presence of two consummate artists exactly in tune with each other.

26 December 1976

That Time, Footfalls, Play

WASHINGTON, D.C. – Samuel Beckett continues on his course of distillation, reducing art to essence. He has never wasted movement or words – he can say more with less than any other contemporary writer – but his most recent plays are even shorter, more austere, more intense. In *Not I* (presented in 1972 at Lincoln Centre), a character is represented by a mouth: a woman's crimson lips, spotlighted, trapped in a frenzied confession. *That Time* and *Footfalls*, his two newest plays, which received their American premiere in the Kreeger Theatre at Washington's Arena Stage, are equally spare and pure, a further refining and defining of this supreme artist's stark vision.

In *That Time*, the head of a man, surrounded by a corona of white hair, appears to be floating, disembodied, in space. Occasionally, the eyes open and close. The man breathes, but the head is largely immobile. The man is silent, but we hear his voice, emerging from three different places on the stage. Each voice reminds him of a crucial, even traumatic, moment in his life. One tells about a ruin of a building where he hid as a child and to which he returned as an adult. The second describes a day in an endless winter when he took shelter from the rain in a musty museum and found himself alone with 'portraits of the dead'. The third is a pastoral idyll of love in the radiant sun.

Childhood, education or history, romance – the three stories flow through the blackness of the stage until they become a tapestry of memory. Is the man dead, dying, sleeping? We never know – and perhaps neither does he. Ritualistically he keeps telling himself 'old tales to keep the

145

void from pouring in' on top of him. He is a man entombed in the abyss of his life.

In the ghostly *Footfalls*, a middle-aged woman, old and worn beyond her years, paces the stage, nine steps then turnabout, nine steps, then turnabout. She also walks in her mind, talking to her aged, sick mother (who talks but does not appear). The woman's story is mysterious. She has not been outdoors since childhood. She is a drudging nurse to her mother's infirmity, and she is also knotted to her own past. Something – we never find out what – has stained her, has consigned her to this carefully measured existence. 'Will you never have done . . . revolving it all . . . in your mind?' asks the mother.

Both plays are interior monologues. The words seem to tumble directly from the subconscious. They seem disoriented, but, listening, wafted on a lyrical tide of images, we find an order and a poetry. Each play is a litany of the elusiveness of remembrance. Why do we remember certain moments and forget others? What draws the curtain on our memory screen? These anguished souls, enduring the redundancy of their days, seek in their past for anchors. These are night plays, dark dreams in which past, present and future are intertwined.

The plays – strange, hypnotic and exquisite – are organically linked with Beckett's other works. The man in *That Time* is an older Krapp, except in this case the tape recorder is in his mind (there is nothing mechanical or even scenic on stage) playing back an endless transcription. He tries to understand the nature of turning points, to find self-expression before his words dry up. The woman in *Footfalls* is a sister to Winnie, who was buried up to her neck in earth in *Happy Days*, and to the woman in *Not I*. All are trapped in a reflexive routine, a holding pattern. She is will-less, forced to repeat herself in a sharply limited world.

The plays may sound static and undramatic. Actually they are astonishingly visual and theatrical. Although the script is specific, there is no way to imagine how they look on stage.

That Time is like staring into an automobile headlight. The image – that shimmering head – burns our eyes (and almost seems to sear our brain). Staring at the white globe on a black field, we began to see hallucinations: man into angel. The head glows, sending off waves. We focus our eyes again until the head becomes a sculpture, an icon.

Footfalls we perceive through the half-light. The stage is dim, the woman's face shrouded by shadows. We see her feet, follow her path and hear her padding steps. The woman's tread is so insistent that it creates its own music: a dirge. It is as if she is walking on her own grave. Just as every movement – the opening of an eye in *That Time*, a turnabout in *Footfalls* – is consequential, the smallest sound can be monumental, and the ringing of chimes becomes cosmic.

I saw the plays in their world premiere engagement at the Royal Court Theatre in London earlier this year during a season of Beckett, with the author himself directing *Footfalls*. At the Arena Stage, Alan Schneider, who is Beckett's watchman as director in America, is particularly fortunate in his choice of Donald Davis for *That Time*. This Canadian actor, who played the title role in the first New York production of *Krapp's Last Tape*, has a marvellously rich voice, with the resonance of an Orson Welles. He is able to modulate his tone so that one can readily distinguish among the three voices in the dark: three instruments playing different songs in harmony.

In London, *Footfalls* was played by the unmatchable Billie Whitelaw. It is a role that requires little acting in the traditional sense, but in the stoop of her body and her movement on stage, Miss Whitelaw managed to suggest the infinite anguish of this tormented woman. Doubled over almost into a right angle, shrouded in rags, Dianne Wiest seems somehow less personal. But she is effective (as is Sloane Shelton, the third performer) and Mr. Davis is exceptional. The lighting and sound are precise. Mr. Schneider's production is an authentic recapitulation of the original.

147

At the Arena as at the Royal Court, the two new short pieces were presented in company with Beckett's earlier *Play*. Written in the early 1960's, *Play* has aged into a classic. It is one of Beckett's most frequently performed and most accessible works. Though the setting is unearthly – three people in funeral urns, their heads so encrusted that they look like decayed corpses – the story is easily identifiable. This is a love triangle, a man, his embittered wife and the other woman. Each recites a monologue, individually and overlapping, the speech triggered by a shifting beam of light as interrogator.

With its pungent cross-currents of insults and marital discord, *Play* has many laughs, but never before has it actually seemed a comedy. As staged by Mr. Schneider, this is a comic curtain-raiser to the unforgettable human agonies of *That Time* and *Footfalls*.

31 March 1977

Waiting for Godot

The definitive production of *Waiting for Godot*, the greatest play of our time, opened Tuesday at the Brooklyn Academy of Music. The only problem for English-speaking audiences is that the performance is in German – a production of West Berlin's Schiller-Theater. It is definitive because it is staged by the author, Samuel Beckett, who, as a director of his own work, has the same precise lucidity of vision that marks his writing.

Beckett clearly sees his play as a human comedy. It is terribly funny as well as tragic, a fact that is communicated in any language, even without words. Never before has *Godot* seemed so extraordinarily visual.

Waiting for Godot is the ultimate statement on man's condition on earth. The pivotal speech belongs to Didi. At the end of the play, he concisely summarises the plot: he and his fellow tramp Gogo have waited, Pozzo has passed, night is falling, and they are still waiting. Then, paraphrasing what he has heard from Pozzo, he says, 'Astride of a grave and a difficult birth . . . we have time to grow old. The air is full of our cries. But habit is a great deadener.'

Life as habit is one Beckett's primary concerns, the routines, rituals and games – the waiting – that we go through in the name of survival. Repeatedly in his production themes are evoked, not just in words, but in facial expressions, hand movements, body positions and places on stage occupied by the actors. Didi and Gogo are opposites, two halves of one person. Beckett accentuates the contrast and the symbiosis. He has said that he thinks of Didi as a tree, Gogo as a rock, an attitude that is eloquently elucidated in the performance. This is ensemble acting of the very highest order.

Didi (Stefan Wigger) is as spindly as a spruce. His eyes are knot-holes and his arms are uneven branches. Gogo (Horst Bollmann) is not only a rock, he is a stump. He is earthy; Didi is airy. Each character would like to be the other. With scarecrow feet, Didi walks pigeon-toed, knees pressed together. He is trying to be earthbound. Gogo walks duck-footed, splaying his feet. He springs when he moves, churning his arms like a windmill. He would like to fly.

In many productions, Gogo becomes the clown and Didi is something of a straight man. Here they are a perfectly balanced team of exquisite comic artists. Mr. Wigger is Tati to Mr. Bollmann's Chaplin. Perhaps it was Ray Bolger who should have been matched with Bert Lahr in the 1956 Broadway version. One of the many lessons learned in this moving performance is that there has to be the closest kinship between the two principal actors. These are friends for life. Mr. Bollmann and Mr. Wigger act as if they had antenna to each other's soul.

Of course there is another pair in *Godot*, Pozzo and Lucky, master and servant. Carl Raddatz's Pozzo is the most obviously Germanic figure on stage – stolid and officious. Lucky (Klaus Herm), the obedient slave who runs his master, delivers his fantastic monologue not as a madman's harangue but as a last desperate attempt to communicate.

The exactness of the script and the performance is reflected in Matias's sets and costumes and Heinz Hohenwald's lighting. There is an almost Oriental simplicity about the production. Knowing German would help one's appreciation, but, more importantly, one should know the play. For anyone who wants to understand this masterpiece – certainly for any actor, director or designer who is contemplating doing *Godot* – this fabulous production is an essential experience.

14 January 1980

Endgame

Blind, lame, confined to a throne-like chair, Hamm exists in a space out of time, measuring the minutes and the minutiae of his life as if they are a spiralling heap of sand. Hamm is himself 'a speck in the void'. The view from his outpost, a bunker in a world facing apocalypse, is bleak in the extreme: no rescue, no salvation and, apparently, no end to death in life. *Endgame* is a tragedy, but it is also a desperate comedy. As Hamm's mother, Nell, says, 'Nothing is funnier than unhappiness, I grant you that.'

Endgame lacks the physical playfulness of Beckett's other masterwork, *Waiting for Godot*. In contrast, it seems relatively inanimate. Hamm sits. His servant, Clov, moves mechanically. His parents, Nagg and Nell, are stumps of people entrapped in ashcans. However, there is linear movement within the text as well as a density of poetic language. *Endgame* demands a virtuoso performance, which is what it receives from Daniel Seltzer, the Hamm of Joseph Chaikin's authoritative production of the play, which opened last night at the Manhattan Theatre Club.

Mr. Chaikin and Mr. Seltzer never forget the play's portent, but neither do they shortchange its mordant humour. The director approaches *Endgame* as a game to be played, as a piece to be performed. Mr. Chaikin is an experimental artist who is scrupulous when dealing with classics. This is an authentic *Endgame* down to the last agitated pause.

In performance, *Endgame* is encountered on an infinite number of planes – as a study of the master-servant relationship, as a child's response to parental abuse, as a play about the winnowing of time and humanity, the lengthening of life, the ending of the world. It is a game of chess, a battle of wits, a homage to Shakespeare.

As his name implies, Hamm is something of an actor. Mr. Seltzer, clothed like a bedraggled monarch, acts up to suit the occasion. He flares from contemplation to bluster, making excessive drill-sergeant demands on his bonded servant. Mr. Seltzer's Hamm is not simply magisterial, he is billy-goat-gruff. For all his petulance, he communicates a sardonic self-awareness of the role that he is playing.

When he comments, 'Our revels now are ended,' the reference to *The Tempest* is not casual but resonant. This Hamm is a Prospero who has given up his staff of magic. Past retirement, he is waiting impatiently for his death. Clov is his complaining Caliban, unable to obey his own impulse toward freedom, serving his unreasonable master because that is what is expected of him and because Hamm keeps the combination to the kitchen cupboard. For Clov, Hamm represents father and sustainer.

Hamm is also tied to his own fate. As he says to himself, 'The end is in the beginning and yet you go on.' One solace is memory. When Mr. Seltzer asserts, 'I love the old questions,' or tosses off a remembered aside as 'No phone calls?', it is with a comic fervour and bedazzlement that remind one of Bert Lahr.

Ten years ago Mr. Chaikin played Hamm for the Open Theatre, and, listening closely to Mr. Seltzer, one can recognise certain shared rhythms and shadings. The primary differences are in Mr. Seltzer's voice, which has the timbre of a classical tragedian, and his looks, which are like those of a bearded Old Testament prophet – with a twinkle. When he announces, 'I'm warming up for my last soliloquy,' it is as if he is spraying his throat and tuning his tonsils to conquer an obstreperous bit of verse – and an audience. The performance is, in all respects, exemplary.

Michael Gross's Clov is a contrast in face, physique and manner: tall and lean with a look of clownish abashment. His eyes are X's in a cartoon strip. Walking in flopping flapjack boots, he is a cousin to Chaplin. He plays Fool to Hamm's Lear, as well as Caliban to his Prospero and Lucky to his Pozzo. Behind his master's back, he is often imitative and gently derisive. This Clov has more personality than is often the case. Mr. Gross is a wily servant, a scamp in the guise of a simpleton. Together, as self-serving king and knightly slave, Mr. Seltzer and Mr. Gross are a peerless tragicomic couple.

The play's two other characters, Nagg and Nell, stay bottled up in their bins, pleading for their pap and remembering without regret their maltreatment of their son, Hamm. Mr. Chaikin and his designer, Sally Jacobs, offer one ingenious variation on these stoppered parents. Instead of being in separate round cans, they share a rectangular double bin, a trash box built for two.

James Barbosa, who was Nagg to Mr. Chaikin's own Hamm, plays the old man as a niggling, ill-tempered whiner, in contrast to Joan MacIntosh's child-like Nell. In the actress's good-natured portrait, Nell is like a sketch for Winnie in *Happy Days*. Contemplating these unregenerate remnants of his despised biography, Hamm proclaims 'The old folks at home!' Mr. Seltzer turns the line into a thunderclap of laughter.

Hamm wants to get on with his dying, and when Clov spies a young boy outside the window, Hamm is horrified at the idea of life going on. Having already cursed the universe as well as his own progenitor, he is in no mood for rejuvenation. Covering his face with his handkerchief, Mr. Seltzer sits back on his throne, a king almost in check, and continues his infernal waiting. The play is profound. The acting is prodigious.

12 April 1981

Rockaby

BUFFALO – The central image is spellbinding in Samuel Beckett's new play, *Rockaby*, which had its world premiere last week at the Centre for Theatre Research. The play, directed by Alan Schneider, was presented by the State University of New York, in celebration of Beckett's 75th birthday. In *Rockaby*, an old woman, played by Billie Whitelaw, dressed in a black sequined gown, sits in a spotlight in a rocking chair and rocks herself back into memory. Memory is life, and when the river of the woman's subconscious runs dry, the chair stops, her eyes close and she expires. Contradicting a last spasm of rage against futility, an almost beatific, childlike innocence floods the woman's face. It is a moment of transfiguration.

The play lasts only 15 minutes, but by any measure other than length this is a major dramatic event, evocatively encapsulating – in words and in visual metaphor – the perdurability of the human spirit, man's clinging to his mind as life preserver.

Miss Whitelaw, making her long-awaited debut on the American stage, plays two roles – the woman who rocks and the offstage voice that shrouds her in a litany of autobiography. The woman speaks sparsely, urging the voice to respond; occasionally she echoes the words. 'More,' says Miss Whitelaw, figuratively pushing a starter button. The voice begins, then fades and pauses. 'More!' she prods, the repetition of the command becoming increasingly fearful until it is a cry for sustenance and survival. It is a cry that reminds one of the lament of Nagg, the legless father stashed in an ashcan in *Endgame* and pleading for his daily sugar-plum.

As an intuitive emotional experience, *Rockaby* is over-powering, hypnotising the audience in its spotlighted gaze, but, in common with all of Beckett's plays, it also has narrative and intellectual substance, some of it subliminal.

The play charts a woman's journey back into life before she arrives at death. The story is divided into four sections. Sitting in her dead mother's chair and wearing her mother's funereal garment, Miss Whitelaw looks back to her perambulatory days, going 'to and fro', Beckett's shorthand for the circumnavigations, emotional as well as geographic, in everyday life. She is searching futilely for human contact, for 'another creature like herself'. Then she moves inside a house and sits at a window facing a window. She sees a face in the window, a face like hers with 'famished eyes'. It is perhaps her own reflection or a portrait of her mother. In the final scene she retreats to a room, and at the 'close of a long day', assuming the role of her mother, she rocks herself into eternal sleep.

From the opening second, we cannot avert our eyes from the actress and her 'famished eyes'. The image is as strong as flaming red lips in *Not I*, the disembodied head with its white corona of hair in *That Time*, and the woman's ritualist pacing in *Footfalls*, a mother-and-daughter play that Beckett wrote expressly for Miss Whitelaw and that is a kind of prelude to *Rockaby*.

As we watch Miss Whitelaw in the new play, we are engulfed by her voice on tape. The actress crisply enunciates every syllable, measuring her pauses for dramatic effect, finding poetic variety in the repetition of monosyllables. Although most of the text is recorded, as the actress rocks and reacts to the voice, this is very much a live performance piece. Reading it, one can have no idea of its impact on stage. As director, Mr. Schneider, with his customary fidelity to the author, has eloquently articulated Beckett's instructions.

Rockaby exactly suits its length. It distils an experience and extends our imagination. Because the play lasts about as along as the average intermission, Mr. Schneider and his associates have prefaced it with a reading by Miss Whitelaw of a Beckett short story, *Enough.*

The 25-minute reading serves a purpose of contrast and of anticipation. We see Miss Whitelaw at a lectern in her natural guise before she hides her beauty behind old age, and we listen to her read a first-person comic monologue. *Enough* is a grotesquerie and a romance between indeterminate partners, perhaps a young woman and an elderly man. He is so strange and deformed that he may be an extra-terrestrial creature. The piece has an abundant flow of language and a bizarre humour, both of which are communicated by the unerring actress.

During the intermission, she transforms herself, returning to inhabit our memory. The activity of rocking tantalises our minds, with all that it signifies from birth to death: a cradle, a lullaby, a rocking horse and finally the insistent but silent rhythm of the chair itself, which becomes a kind of imaginary vehicle as the character rides out the rest of her life.

31 July 1983
Ohio Impromptu,
Catastrophe, What Where

In his art, Samuel Beckett pursues a course of courageous and pragmatic pessimism. Despite personal dilemmas and public calamities, man strives onward, adapting himself to each crisis and devising methods of endurance. In his latest fiction, *Worstward Ho*, Beckett urges, 'Try again. Fail again. Fail better.' From his point of view, the destination is unavoidable but the journey can be alleviated. For the past 25 years, since *Krapp's Last Tape*, he has been distilling his vision, bringing his theatre and his fiction into closer proximity and writing plays for one or two voices, a speaker and a silent listener or sentinel. Often these are two aspects of one persona. In some of the plays we do even see a whole man or woman: the incessantly moving lips of the woman in *Not I*; the disembodied head surrounded by a flaring corona of white hair in *That Time*. In others we glimpse an isolated figure in limbo: the daughter calculating her steps in *Footfalls*. Though these plays are brief, some lasting a scant 15 minutes, in performance the effect can be awesome – a biographical time line refined into a single mesmerising image.

While all his recent short pieces have had a unity of expression, in his last few plays there is a sign of increasing experimentation. In *Rockaby*, for example, the woman's soliloquy is counterpointed by the sound and the rhythm of her chair, endlessly rocking away her minutes on earth. In *A Piece of Monologue*, the speaker has a silent, totemic double, a tall standing lamp with a skull-size white globe. Any second we expect the lamp to speak. In his three newest plays, Off-Broadway at the Harold Clurman Theatre, Beckett continues to explore the dimensions of the short dramatic form. The result is a compelling triptych of disparate plays.

The opening play, *Ohio Impromptu*, a kind of companion piece to *A Piece of Monologue* (each was originally performed by David Warrilow), speaks poetically and with a stunning theatricality about a last love. *Catastrophe*, the evening's centrepiece, is a politically prescient black comedy about man's enslavement by the state. *What Where*, the most enigmatic of the three pieces, is a cryptic gram of truth about the manipulation of man by men.

Ohio Impromptu begins on a brilliantly lighted stage. Two men sit at right angles at a long table. They are dressed identically in long black coats and flowing white wigs. As doubles, they regard each other with silent suspicion. In the centre of the table is a black, wide-brimmed hat such as might be worn by a pilgrim. The character identified as the Reader (David Warrilow) turns the pages of a large volume, fighting the 'old terror of night' to retell a story from the life of his companion and alter ego, identified as the Listener. It is a story about a departed loved one, who haunts the Listener's night thoughts.

Repeatedly the Listener interrupts the monologue with a knock on the table, which acts as punctuation and as a signal for the Reader to stop and to repeat. The Reader polishes his monologue, a self-editing process that itself is a motif in a number of recent Beckett plays, which deal tangentially with the creative process. In a sense, the Reader becomes a kin of Beckett's Krapp. Instead of replaying a tape, he replays a story with stops and starts. Eventually he arrives at the end, 'the sad tale a last time told'. In Beckett's own case, the telling never ceases. Stories, like footfalls, keep returning, with variations on variations, and in *Ohio Impromptu*, with images that sear our memory.

Of the three plays, *Catastrophe* is the most elaborate and the most tangible. It takes place on a real stage, with scenery, contemporary costumes and an exchange of pungent dialogue. The play is dedicated to Václav Havel, the dissident Czechoslovak playwright, and was first presented in France as part of a festival honouring Havel. It is the most overt expression of Beckett's political consciousness, his compassionate testimony about the cause of human rights. To some degree, the piece represents a return for the author to the verbal playfulness of his earlier dramatic work. For all its mordancy, *Catastrophe* remains a comedy, albeit one on a most oppressive theme.

The scene is a stage being prepared for a public performance, such as one might encounter in an Iron Curtain country or in ancient Rome. A man, as bony as a cadaver, stands helplessly on a plinth, a prisoner in the dock awaiting sentence. He is identified as the Protagonist (hauntingly personified by Mr. Warrilow). The Director, who is both a theatrical deviser and the representative of a police state, orders a female assistant to rearrange the Protagonist's limbs, features and clothes. He is moulded as if he were clay on the way to becoming a statue of suffering. The figure is meant to serve as a death's head warning to others who might dare to follow him into an act of rebellion.

The Director (Kevin O'Connor, who replaced Donald Davis in the role) is depicted as an overbearing bureaucrat, a fact deepened by his officious manner and his appearance; in his fur coat and toque he looks like a commissar. He is haughtily dismissive of his aide's suggestions, hurrying to a conclusion so that he can rush to a caucus. Finally satisfied with the one-man tableau, with his reordering of reality for propagandistic effect, the Director allows the victim to be placed on exhibition. We hear distant applause, and the Protagonist stares at his unseen audience.

When the play opened in June, in an attempt to characterise Mr. Warrilow's mournful visage, I wrote that he looked at his audience in abject supplication. When I subsequently met with Beckett in Paris, the playwright carefully corrected this description. He indicated that it was not his intention to have the character make an appeal to the audience. Rather he is meant to cow onlookers into submission through the intensity of his gaze and of his stoicism. In other words, he is a triumphant martyr rather than a sacrificial victim – a far more pointed political and spiritual statement.

Although the political consciousness of *Catastrophe* may come as a surprise to some theatregoers, throughout Beckett's plays there is a concern with individualism in opposition to suppressive authority. Pozzo and Lucky in *Waiting for Godot* and Hamm and Clov in *Endgame* are only the salient examples of masters tyrannising servants. Even within a Beckett void, as in *The Lost Ones*, there are societal differences, rituals and demands of duty. Though he is not primarily a political playwright and has never operated as a polemicist, in his work he has expressed an awareness of the world around him. Alan Schneider, the author's most frequent director in America and the exactingly faithful director of the current trio of plays, remembers once being part of a theatrical symposium in which John Arden, a fervid social playwright, attacked Beckett for being apolitical, for not writing plays about the Algerian crisis. Delivering an irate response, Mr. Schneider said that all Beckett's plays were 'about Algeria', meaning the statement in a metaphorical sense. Taking a cue from the director, one might say that more than one of his current plays is about Václav Havel.

With *Catastrophe* in mind, one turns to the third play, *What Where*, and in context it appears to be another assault on totalitarianism. Four shrouded figures, dimly perceived in the half light, accept orders from the voice of a kind of grand inquisitor who demands that an unseen prisoner be given 'the works'. We are told that the victim 'wept, screamed, begged for mercy', but did not confess, choosing torture over recantation. Offering an alternate, non-political interpretation, Mr. Schneider says that *What Where* is 'about the impossibility of defining the nature of existence'. From that perspective, 'the works' are not a sequence of punishments but the great works of philosophy and literature, which each generation studies in search of universal truth.

Reading the play, one can see the possibility of this interpretation, but it does not negate the work's validity as a provocative political statement. The language that the author employs is that of interrogation, not of education. Witnesses are badgered, and 'the works', whatever they are, are inflicted rather than imparted. The evening ends, appropriately, on a note of mystification, with the voice announcing, 'Make sense who may. I switch off.' Though scholars and critics have been encyclopaedic in their attempts to explicate the works of Beckett, an aesthetic equivalent of what the Director in *Catastrophe* calls 'a craze for explicitation', the author avoids exegesis. At 77, our pre-eminent living playwright continues to ask profound questions and to leave analysis to others.

21 September 1986

Adapting Beckett's Prose

At the same time that Samuel Beckett has been adamant about directors respecting every single line of dialogue and stage direction in his plays, he has allowed surprising latitude to those he trusts in adapting his prose pieces and radio plays into works of theatre. In conversation, he has made the distinction clear. A play is meant to be performed exactly as the playwright wrote it, but a work not originally designed for the theatre can be subject to the interpretation, the visual imagination of the adapter – should the author permit adaptation.

Among primary benefactors of the Beckett largess in this area are members of the Mabou Mines, America's foremost experimental ensemble. The Mabou Mines, which often creates its own original works, has treated Beckett as a kind of house author while rarely performing his actual theatre pieces. Away from Mabou Mines, JoAnne Akalaitis, one of the company's most versatile artists, staged *Endgame* several seasons ago at the American Repertory Theatre in Cambridge, Mass. That elaborative production became the storm centre of the Beckett directorial controversy, with Beckett, through intermediaries, protesting the production. Ten years ago, Ms. Akalaitis, with permission of the author, dramatised his radio play *Cascando* for the Mabou Mines and found her own visual approximation of the auditory experience. She placed the play's characters around a table, such as one might find in a pub and then caused the table to levitate and the people to interact physically. While remaining faithful to the author's words, Ms. Akalaitis's *Cascando* was like an animated Red Grooms environment.

Similarly, Lee Breuer turned *The Lost Ones*, a narrative fragment, into a Mabou Mines performance piece for the actor David Warrilow. The narrative describes the life in limbo of a multitude confined inside a large cylinder. The actor became both the primary denizen of this Dantesque zone and, by aligning minuscule paper cut-outs of his fellow prisoners, he became a Gulliver ex machina.

Of all the current members of the Mabou Mines, Frederick Neumann has been the most concerned with the works of Beckett (Mr. Warrilow, who certainly shares that concern as an actor, is no longer an active member of the troupe). Mr. Neumann has adapted, directed and acted in his versions of *Mercier and Camier*, *Company* and, currently, *Worstward Ho* – and on his own he has appeared as an actor in dramatic works by Beckett. *Worstward Ho* (at the Classic Stage Company) is the first of his three Beckett adaptations that manages the transmutation intact.

The earlier attempts suffered from varying difficulties. As a short novel about two tramps in mudtime, surviving in 'hospitable chaos', *Mercier and Camier* could be regarded as a rough fictional sketch for *Waiting for Godot*. It is too complicated a piece – filled with incident, jump cuts and authorial asides – to be contained easily on stage, especially as a work of chamber theatre. Perhaps it might be treated more effectively in film or on television. In contrast, *Company*, a monologue by a protagonist who projects himself into a dreamlike past, was a more appropriate selection for adaptation. However, as adapter of *Company*, Mr. Neumann was unable to devise a metaphor sizable enough to encompass the various personae within Beckett's single character. As an actor in this piece, he was most comfortable in the few moments of humour, as in his imagining of a housefly as company.

Worstward Ho is a definite indication that Mr. Neumann has grown as adapter, director and actor. Drawing from within Beckett's text and applying his own imagination, he has devised an impressive visual metaphor, placing the narrator (played by himself) in a graveyard. Up to his knees in his grave, the narrator conjures up the sombre figures on Beckett's landscape – a boy and his father hand in hand visiting the cemetery and a stoical maternal figure whom they watch and who watches them. Enhanced by L. B. Dallas's sound system, Mr. Neumann's voice becomes a deeply resonant Beckett instrument. The actor also allows himself a few droll comic moments in this grave context. When he accidently drops a shovel into the tomb, it bounces its way down an endless well, as the narrator watches in abashment.

As demonstrated by the Mabou Mines versions of *Cascando*, *The Lost Ones* and *Worstward Ho*, the most important element in Beckett adaptation – in addition to fidelity to the source – is the discovery of a metaphor or an image, through which one can visualise the original piece. Finding such a conduit to the stage, each of the three adaptations became a worthy addition to Beckett's theatrical body of work. They are, in effect, 'found' plays. This was also the case with Ruth Maleczech's 14-minute holographic adaptation of the Beckett fragment *Imagination Dead Imagine*. With the help of Linda Hartinian, one of many visual artists in residence as designers with the Mabou Mines, Ms. Maleczech approached the text as if it were a sculpture for installation. The central 'character' became a catafalque on which were played beams of light that changed the colour of the stone and also projected images that seemed to float on the surface. Combining light, voice and sounds in rhythmic patterns, the director gave Beckett's own image a striking theatrical setting.

When one considers these successful adaptations, one realises again the close relationship of Beckett's prose and theatre, especially evident in his more recent work in both categories. The prose pieces, *Company* and *Worstward Ho*, are partners in inspiration with Beckett's later monologues, *That Time* through *Rockaby*. With the monologues, of course, Beckett has created his own visual imagery – the disembodied head with a corona of white hair for *That Time*, the old woman in her rocking chair in *Rockaby*. Through some mysterious alchemy, the reader or theatregoer is able to share the author's dream (and subconscious).

Several misconceptions have arisen. The monologues are not necessarily monodramas. Most of the theatrical works are plays for two or more voices, even when those voices come from the same person. The plays are dramatic not circumlocutionary, and they are unified by the relentless flow of Beckett's language and by his underlying sense of poetry. In *On Beckett: Essays and Criticism*, an anthology published this month by Grove Press, one Beckett scholar, Enoch Brater, describes *Rockaby* accurately as 'a performance poem in the shape of a play'. One could say, equally, that *Worstward Ho* is a play in the shape of a poetic piece of fiction. This strong unifying strand between the monologues and the fiction was, some years ago, one of the many aspects of Jack MacGowran's nonpareil evening of selections from the works of Beckett. In one actor's embodiment, one felt the poetic totality of a major artist.

Coincident with the production of *Worstward Ho*, there is an Off-Broadway revival of *Krapp's Last Tape*, starring Rick Cluchey, as directed by Beckett himself. Though Mr. Cluchey is not, in this performance, an actor with the flair of Donald Davis, who created the role of Krapp in the United States, or of Hume Cronyn, who played it at Lincoln Centre, he is a good actor who has profited from his association with the author. He most certainly must be credited with fidelity.

Listen to *Krapp's Last Tape*, and one can hear the authoritative and most poetic voice of Beckett, as Krapp remembers his youthful romantic idyll, sailing on a lake at midnight in the company of his love – a scene of great beauty and, in retrospect, a moment of wistful longing. Hearing this 30-year-old memory of his own happy days, the old Krapp becomes cross. He switches off the tape recording and broods. 'Hard to believe I was ever as bad as that. Thank God that's all done with anyway.' Then, after a pause, he adds about his lost love, 'The eyes she had!' As we listen to the later Beckett of *Worstward Ho*, we can still hear the echoes of young Krapp, of the author's romantic surge, as his speaker plods 'nohow on' into the twilight.

2 April 1989

Radio Plays

Of all Samuel Beckett's dramatic works, the ones that have been most neglected are his radio plays. The major stage plays are continually revived, the television plays are shown with a certain frequency, at least in West Germany, but his work for radio exists largely as printed texts. On the page, they lose half their dimension. With the help of aural tapestry – articulate actors, sound effects and music – disembodied voices achieve visceral embodiment. Listeners are transported into the character's subconscious, complete with visual as well as auditory imagery.

This neglect will be partly rectified by a month-long festival of five Beckett radio plays, broadcast on National Public Radio beginning this week. As produced and directed by Everett C. Frost and featuring a company of esteemed Beckett actors (including, most notably, Barry McGovern, Billie Whitelaw and David Warrilow), the series is a rare opportunity to encounter the author in one of his explorative phases. It is also a chance to realise the imaginative possibilities of radio drama and to experience the benefits of restricting an audience's perception to a single sense.

Beckett first entered radio in 1957, at the suggestion of the BBC. The result was *All That Fall*, written between *Waiting for Godot* and *Endgame*. It is a masterwork worthy of that company. Mr. Frost's production of *All That Fall* (starring Ms. Whitelaw, Mr. Warrilow and Alvin Epstein), broadcast in the United States in 1986 in celebration of the author's 80th birthday, leads off the present festival. The other plays all represent American premieres; they are, in order of broadcast, *Embers*, *Words and Music*, *Cascando* and *Rough for Radio II*.

167

What is most astonishing about the plays is Beckett's intuitive command of the intricacies of the form, immediately evident in *All That Fall*. A vibrant, abundantly populated rustic tale filled with dark humour, it follows the journey – a life's journey in miniature – of old Maddy Rooney (Ms. Whitelaw) to meet her blind husband (Mr. Warrilow) at the train station.

Along the way she encounters a series of dilemmas and momentary disasters. Asking one reluctant woman for her arm as support, Maddy exclaims, 'A helping hand! For five seconds! Christ what a planet!' – lines that ring with comic exasperation. *All That Fall* is one of the author's most expansive works in any medium, and his only radio play that one could also easily imagine on stage or on film.

Embers, first presented by the BBC in 1959, is an exceedingly complex interior monologue, delivered by a man alone on a beach. In it, the protagonist, Henry, spins himself back into memory and imagination, conversing with his wife and his father (a suicide on that beach many years ago). Henry conjures up sounds as well as characters – the beating of waves, the clatter of horses' hooves – repeating them like favourite old tunes. In common with many of Beckett's later stage plays, *Embers* deals with the dying of life, the emptiness of life without love or company and with laughter in the face of despair.

From it, one can gather Henry's autobiography, that of a boy disregarded by his father (whose last words to his son were, 'You're a washout'). Henry himself has become an abusive father and a neglectful husband. But as we hear about the others in his world, we begin to understand the character's psychic disorders and the roots of resultant cynicism. Mr. McGovern enriches the role with subtly shaded, occasionally thunderous emotions and a resonant Irish timbre, an ideal complement to the sound of the sea in the background. In a note of authenticity, the waves were taped on location at Killiney Beach, just south of Dublin.

Mr. McGovern's laughter is itself a tour de force as he rallies his voice, gropes, rasps, cackles and then issues, as

Beckett's stage directions demand, a 'long horrible laugh,' which seems to rattle from the grave. It is quickly followed by the droll question, 'Any of the old charm there?' The original BBC production was apparently marred by inaudibility. Mr. Frost's version is a brilliant act of reclamation.

The title characters in *Words and Music*, the most virtuosic piece in the festival, are humorously addressed as Joe and Bob. Joe is portrayed by Mr. Warrilow, Bob by a seven-piece orchestra playing a score by Morton Feldman. Ordering words and music into play is the third character, Croak (Mr. Epstein). In his arrogance, Croak suggests the figure of Pozzo in *Waiting for Godot*, as he demands that his two servants work 'together, dogs'.

The play is an intense depiction of the difficulty of the artistic process, which Croak tries to will into action. Joe has a tendency to be rhetorical, Bob to be sentimental. Eventually meshed, they create two touching songs, one about love, the other about age.

Cascando, one radio play that has been performed in the theatre (it was staged by JoAnne Akalaitis in 1976), deals with a similar theme. A Voice (Mr. Epstein in the current version) tries to finish telling a story about a character in flight, while Music (a score by William Kraft) completes its own composition.

Rough for Radio II carries the analysis of creativity into political areas. In that sense, it is a precursor of the late Beckett stage play, *Catastrophe*. In *Rough for Radio II,* an Animator (W. Dennis Hunt), assisted by a Stenographer (Amanda Plummer) and a mute lackey with a whip, tries to force a man named Fox (Mr. McGovern) into writing. (In the BBC production, these roles were played by Harold Pinter, Billie Whitelaw and Patrick Magee.) Fox is helpless but resistant, proving that inspiration cannot be manipulated. What it needs is 'a wellhead' – a source or inspiration, such as Beckett himself draws from in his work.

One has a single small reservation about the radio festival. The introductory commentary is simplistic, although the

169

accompanying discussions by Beckett critics and scholars are informative. Technically as well as dramatically, the five plays speak for themselves as exemplars of the radio art. In the phrase that the critic Martin Esslin once used to describe *Words and Music*, Beckett's radio plays are 'totally radiogenic'. Listening to them, one receives a mind's-eye view of an entire Beckett cosmos.

13 October 1990

Happy Days

Despite her cheerful demeanour, Winnie in *Happy Days* (revived at the Classic Stage Company) knows the limits and defeats of her life. Her way to endure the day, and the day after that, is 'laughing wild amid severest woe'. Laughter shares the stage with sorrow.

As Winnie (Charlotte Rae) primps and fusses over herself, it is as if she is sitting at her dressing table. She is, of course, buried up to her waist in a large mound of earth and, by the second act of Samuel Beckett's masterly existential comedy, she is buried up to her neck. In the unwritten third act, she might have become the distant voice of someone symbolically entombed in life.

Peggy Ashcroft has called the role 'a summit part', like Hamlet. Any actress attempting it must find her path through a minefield of detailed stage directions and must single-handedly sustain the drama. Although her husband, Willie, appears, he seldom speaks, leaving the stage to his wife and her one-woman show. Necessarily the role lends itself to interpretation, but no performance should neglect the essential adaptability of Winnie. Though her stage movements are rigidly restricted, emotionally she is unbound.

In Carey Perloff's thoughtful production, Ms. Rae holds firmly to the author's inclinations – the pauses, stops and starts and poetic lilt of language. With an ebullience that seems to spring from conviction, she goes about her everyday life, undeterred by the fact of her entrapment. This is a Winnie who is unswerving in her ability to come through wars as well as personal deprivations.

171

Best known for her comic performances, Ms. Rae aims for lightness and achieves it as called for in the first act, which benefits from the actress's expressive face and gestures. She also catches a measure of the second act sobriety, when Winnie's soliloquy begins to resemble the delirium of later Beckett works like *Not I*.

For the audience, she becomes a cosy chatterer such as one might encounter in an English pub. She engages us with her refrain, as she tries to recall happy beginnings as well as endings. Other actresses from Ruth White in the original Off-Broadway production to Irene Worth have uncovered the gentility beneath the extroverted behaviour. That aspect of Winnie eludes Ms. Rae, who is most adept at projecting the character's earthy humour.

At the CSC, the audience is seated on three sides of a small stage. Donald Eastman's set places Winnie in the centre of a volcano-like hill. The surface looks seared. In the close surroundings Ms. Rae keeps her performance within the framework of intimacy. Bill Moor is apt as Willie, her crusty companion, in top hat and tails looking like a remnant from another, more formal epoch.

Ms. Perloff previously directed *Happy Days* (with Ms. Rae and Mr. Moor) at the Mark Taper Forum in Los Angeles as part of that company's recent retrospective of plays of the 1950's and 1960's. The production arrives here with a sense of surety, except in one respect. In a sudden flash, Winnie's parasol is supposed to be consumed by flames, but when the moment came during a critics' preview, the fire fizzled. Spontaneous combustion resulted in a puff of smoke.

The director and the actress are careful about keeping the dialogue conversational, even when it is alluding to Milton, Dante and Shakespeare. Ever eclectic, Winnie remembers literary references as a kind of artifact of a cultural heritage she does not possess.

Because of Winnie's persistence, some may regard her as an eternal optimist. Her role is more that of perpetual pragmatist. As she passes the minutes with remembered routines and favourite distractions, *Happy Days* becomes a partial reflection of *Waiting for Godot*. Neither salvation nor cessation await her; one dawn is like another. Searchingly, Winnie looks for daily mercies as her helpmate for survival.

2 November 1992

Texts for Nothing

Rising from a crouching position, the tramp surveys his
surroundings, a mysterious environment of overlapping
planks, and wonders where he is. As Samuel Beckett's *Texts
for Nothing* unfolds (at the Joseph Papp Public Theatre), we
can sense that the man is trapped in limbo. Perhaps the last
man on earth, he is hanging on for life while waiting for a
'desinence,' a Beckettian word meaning an end, as in the end
of a sentence. He has no idea when it will come. But until it
comes, he is 'a prisoner, frantic with corporeality'. As he
says, 'I can't stay. I can't go,' adds with curiosity, 'Let's see
what happens next.'

This prose piece, 13 terse chapters of a fiction, followed on
stage by a coda extracted from the novel *How It Is*, is a distillation of the author's art and philosophy. Therefore it is
fitting that the dramatisation of *Texts for Nothing* is given an
astonishing performance by Bill Irwin, a clown in an intense
tragi-comic mode.

With Mr. Irwin alone with Beckett's words and thoughts,
the 65-minute play says more about man's misfortunes than
many plays do in double or triple the time. The performance
offers an acting lesson in how Beckett's prose can be transformed into theatre.

When the piece was first staged in 1981, the actor was
Joseph Chaikin. (The adaptation is by Mr. Chaikin and
Steven Kent.) The new production is scrupulously directed by
Mr. Chaikin. Beckett's primal themes are all in place: his
cogitation of the brief abyss between birth and death, his
reflections on man's inability to ascertain his place in the cosmos. Mr. Irwin's character seeks to name what is unnamable,

using a blanket of precise words to prove that words are useless.

On the page this is a haunting interior monologue. On stage, it is both internalised and externalised, moving deeply within the meaning of the prose and also contemplating the subtext, including the kinship between the writer and his character. Shifting from perplexity to wonderment to despair, the actor breathes a visceral actuality into the nightmare. Led by Mr. Irwin, the audience enters that nightmare, as he feels his way around the 'inextricable place' searching for a foot-hold and a mind hold.

A word about the setting: Christine Jones has artfully detailed the wooden landscape (like the interior of a hull of a Viking ship) with hidden crevasses in which Mr. Irwin can amusingly lose himself, or his hat. When he finds that hat, he flips it onto his head and smiles with satisfaction, one of the few moments in which he allows himself a clownish gesture. Along with other Beckett actors like Bert Lahr and Buster Keaton, Mr. Irwin is a masterly clown and mime. He punctu-ates his words with expressive looks and animates his nimble limbs with a dancer's agility. With him, the visual and perfor-mance elements assume equal weight with the text.

With wide-ranging resourcefulness, the actor illuminates the complex narrative, whether he is using his hands to measure the length of an hour or a century (arms stretching elastically across the stage) or miming the ages of man, playing a feeble 'Old Tot' reaching high into the air to grasp his nanny's arm for support. When the character talks to his body, the actor becomes his own puppeteer, activating his arms and legs. Searching for a resting position on this unyielding landscape, he sits, lies down, discovers the alternative of kneeling and finds no comfort. Called upon to conjure other characters, he achieves a kaleidoscopic diversity: the scene of a father telling his son a ghoulish bedtime story turns into small two-character comedy.

In his original performance in the role, Mr. Chaikin assumed a childlike air, retaining his boyishness even as he aged. Maintaining a related aura of innocence, Mr. Irwin pitches his voice in the range of Mr. Chaikin's. When he is briefly heard on tape, acting as his subconscious, the tone is deeper. The seedy figure, wearing vest and spats to denote his once dapper existence, is marked by his world-weariness and word-weariness. Has not everything been said, he scolds his author. Through his approach, Mr. Irwin brings the character closer to other Beckett tramps, like Mercier and Camier and Didi and Gogo themselves. In his sombre introspection about his 'old wander years', about what he has lost in his life, there are also aspects of *Krapp's Last Tape*.

Hugh Kenner has summarised the events in *Texts for Nothing* as 'fantasies of non-being'. Mr. Irwin makes the fantasies corporeal without losing any of their fanciful context. Although he does not have the resonant voice of a Jack MacGowran, he is in total command of Beckett's 'pell-mell Babel of silence and words'. In performance he offers stunning still pictures as well as tragi-comedy in motion.

In Mike Nichols's Lincoln Centre production of *Waiting for Godot*, Mr. Irwin delivered Lucky's monologue with staccato brilliance. With *Texts for Nothing*, he spurs a theatregoer's anticipation for more of the actor's explorations into the world of Beckett.

7 March 1993
The Theatrical Notebooks
of Samuel Beckett

VOLUME TWO: *Endgame*
VOLUME THREE: *Krapp's Last Tape*

In our many conversations over the years, Samuel Beckett was always reluctant to discuss the meaning and philosophy behind his work, preferring to stand on the principle of no exegesis where none intended. When pressed, he would talk about the genesis of individual plays and about production and performance. As it turns out, production and performance were central to his concept of his art. Years after he began writing plays, he became an active participant in the theatrical process and a consummate director of his own work. What began as an act of utmost privacy reached into the rehearsal room, where the author, watching actors play his roles, would distil and clarify his plays.

While directing his plays in Germany and England, Beckett kept production notebooks, which are being published in facsimile form together with his final revised texts of the plays. The first volumes of *The Theatrical Notebooks of Samuel Beckett* deal with *Endgame* and *Krapp's Last Tape*. The notebook on *Waiting for Godot*, though labelled Volume One, is scheduled to be published in England this spring, and a book on the shorter plays will follow. Beckett himself was actively involved in the project, in the case of *Endgame* and *Krapp's Last Tape* going over the text line by line with the editors. With the publication of the notebooks, we now have a more authoritative view of both the art and the artist.

S. E. Gontarski, the editor of the *Endgame* notebook, says, 'Beckett discovered that theatre allowed him to paint (or sculpt), that is, to work directly with form'. As is abundantly clear from these volumes, Beckett's art underwent a continuing evolutionary process. Just as museum conservators use infra-red instruments to study paintings and to reveal underlying aspects of an artist's creative process, James Knowlson – who is the general editor of the series as well as the editor of the *Krapp's Last Tape* volume – and Mr. Gontarski use their infra-red scholarship to uncover the pentimento behind the plays.

The editors, both of whom are Beckett scholars, decipher Beckett's handwriting (in English, French and German) and even read beneath his erasures. The texts are densely documented and footnoted, an approach that could have led to a dissection of minutiae. Instead, it leads to illumination.

Although directors have published production logbooks, it is rare that a playwright provides such material. Beckett's notebooks bring us closer to the author's mind and, tangentially, to his life. We can see his careful, deliberative method and his serious concern for structure. Those who think of him solely as an intuitive artist will be surprised at the meticulous quality of his writing, self-editing and rewriting. At the same time, it is evident that he was neither dogmatic nor didactic. As Mr. Knowlson says in a prefatory note, 'The material reveals a flexibility and an openness of approach that is often considered alien to Beckett's way of working in the theatre.' Appropriately, the editor views the plays as a 'living organism', not as works cast in stone.

Although Beckett wanted to protect his work from deconstructionists, he allowed for a certain amount of directorial (and actorial) interpretation, his own as well as that of others. The journals offer Beckett in purest form, with an added aspect of mystery, of literary sleuthing, as the editors lead us into the intricacies of the author's choices. We might be sitting next to Beckett as he explores and learns about his work.

Some of the material in these volumes has been previously available in books like *Beckett in the Theatre*, by Dougald McMillan and Martha Fehsenfeld, and Mr. Knowlson's *Theatre Workbook* on *Krapp's Last Tape*. The current publication brings together a wealth of information in a finely detailed and highly readable format. These notebooks add to the expanding Beckett library, which now also includes the early, previously unpublished novel, *Dream of Fair to Middling Women*. That book, published late last year in Dublin, is scheduled to be brought out here by Arcade Publishing in the spring.

So many of the alterations in the plays derive from Beckett's impatience, his apparent urge to make the performance flow more swiftly and precisely. Dialogue is cut and actions are added. In the revised *Endgame*, Clov the servant is more physically active; Hamm the master yawns less. In his stage directions, Beckett specifies more clearly the moods and reactions of his characters while also stressing the significance of aural and visual imagery as well as motifs. Both plays seem funnier, though less clownish. Hamm is no longer described as having a very red face, and Krapp does not have a purple nose or trousers that are too short. There is more attention to Krapp's attachment to his tape recorder and less stage business with bananas. The title character does not sing 'Now the Day Is Over', because Beckett felt the singing was self-conscious. These changes are part of a larger scheme in which Beckett analyses the intimations he has aroused and communicates them more evocatively to the audience. In all respects, he expands the dimensions of his theatre.

Beckett said that the line 'Nothing is funnier than unhappiness' was the most important sentence in *Endgame*. Reading the author's notebook, one can see an increasing emphasis on the play as a comedy of pessimism, with the comedy contradicting the dourness of some productions by other directors. Similarly, in *Krapp* he pointed to the line 'The earth might be uninhabited' as pivotal. That line denotes Krapp's abject isolation, his 'incarceration in self', as a man unable to escape his past and equally unable to comfort himself in the present. Krapp is, in Beckett's words, a 'dream-consumed man'. Although most of Beckett's changes were made for clarity, in at least one instance he was moved by discretion. In *Endgame*, Hamm originally said, 'I feel a little queer'. At the request of the actor Patrick Magee, Beckett changed 'queer' to 'strange'.

The book on *Krapp* is particularly instructive, because the play is so brief, self-contained and autobiographical. It is also the play with which Beckett was most involved in production. A scant eight pages in the present edition, *Krapp* is parsed in the editor's notes for every undercurrent. It is one of the few Beckett pieces inspired by an actor, in this case Magee. Drawn by his mellifluous voice, the author initially referred to the play as 'Magee Monologue'. Beckett was also drawn by his own curiosity about the tape recorder, realising that he could use it as mechanical equivalent of a photographic album, as a way to transport the character back to his past. The tape recorder could have proved to be a problem in performance; the actor playing the title role has to turn it on and off, forward and backward, exactly on cue. The machine, we are told, is generally operated by an offstage assistant and not by the actor on stage.

There is a triple-edged quality to the reflections as Krapp at the age of 69 listens to himself at 39 commenting on his even more youthful self. Two scenes are crucial to an understanding of *Krapp*. An epiphany is experienced by the character (as it was in life by Beckett) standing at night on the jetty at Dun Laoghaire and witnessing a life-transforming 'memorable equinox'. Listening to the tape conjuring that event, Krapp now has a 'violent reaction'. Equally important is the boating scene, in which the speaker recalls a single romantic interlude and bids 'farewell to love.' In the revised version, Krapp 'wipes dream away with hand, broods, shudders'. Throughout the revisions, made over a period of years, Beckett underlined the play's three primary themes, 'solitude, light-darkness and woman' – and in *Endgame*, depletion and deterioration. And in a curious personal note, for one production of *Krapp* Beckett brought in his own bedroom slippers for the actor to wear. He wanted him to have the proper shuffle.

In his notebooks, Beckett assiduously warns against stylisation and sentimentality. As he said during a production of *Endgame*: 'I would like as much laughter as possible in this play. It is a playful piece.' An observer interpreted this as meaning 'laughter of his characters, not the audience's amusement', though, of course, one would lead to the other. Directors of *Endgame* and *Krapp's Last Tape* would certainly benefit from using *The Theatrical Notebooks* as production guides. They are invaluable maps of Beckett country.

25 June 1995
Eleutheria

The abandoned manuscript of Samuel Beckett's first play, *Eleutheria*, has finally found its way into print after a highly dramatic legal and literary battle, with protective executors and eager publishers all insisting they were acting in the author's interest. The conflict continues. The primary question: Are the presumed wishes of the artist more important than the validity of the art?

In 1950, Roger Blin, the French director and actor, was offered Beckett's first two plays, *Eleutheria* and *Waiting for Godot*, for production. He chose the second partly because it had a cast of five and the simplest of settings. With its large cast, *Eleutheria* (which means freedom in Greek) would have demanded a far more expansive staging. After it was produced, *Waiting for Godot* became the seminal play in the contemporary theatre, while *Eleutheria* languished in Beckett's trunk and, later, in scholarly archives, with his own comment attached: 'Prior to Godot. 1947. Unpublished. Jettisoned.'

Last September, Barney Rosset, for many years Beckett's publisher in the United States, presented the first public reading of the play, and then announced his intention of publishing it. In response, Jérôme Lindon, Beckett's literary executor, quickly brought out an edition in the original French, and wrote an introduction attacking Mr. Rosset and, in the name of Beckett, disclaiming the play. The American edition, which has an English translation by Michael Brodsky, a novelist heavily influenced by Beckett, has a series of prefatory remarks by the lawyer Martin Garbus and others defending the play.

It is clear from the manuscript, as it was from the public reading, that *Eleutheria* merits both publication and production, but it must be placed in perspective. If it had been staged before *Godot*, it certainly would not have had the same international impact, though one would have looked forward to the author's next play. *Waiting for Godot* is revolutionary, *Eleutheria* is evolutionary.

As was also true of *Dream of Fair to Middling Women*, Beckett's first novel, published posthumously in 1993, *Eleutheria* fills an important gap in the writer's career. Its value rests partly on the fact that it presages his subsequent plays, in particular *Waiting for Godot* and *Krapp's Last Tape*. However, as a bourgeois comedy with a darkly sardonic heart, it has its own authority and impudent wit. Those who regard Beckett primarily as a minimalist may be surprised by the ebullience of his first play.

In each of the three acts, Beckett experimented with theatrical styles and stage devices. The anti-hero of the play, Victor Krap (an early semblance of the title character in *Krapp's Last Tape*), is a failed writer who has retreated from life. The first act, which takes place in the home of Victor's parents, is a vaudevillised French farce. Victor's fiancée, friends and relatives vehemently object to his self-imposed 'sordid inertia'. At the same time, they also engage in a Feydeau-like roundelay of jealousy and threatened dalliance.

As the scene shifts to Victor's dreary digs, Beckett finds his own voice. The play becomes deeply pessimistic about the pursuit of privacy while remaining antic about the intrusions inflicted on a stubborn individual. After Victor heaves a shoe through a window, a garrulous glazier magically appears as a deus ex machina. With its undertones of *Godot*, the second act could stand alone as an absurdist comedy. Both sets are supposed to remain on stage during the first two acts. Then, in an impossible stage direction, the Krap family home is 'swallowed up' by the orchestra pit. The third act adds a touch of Pirandello as a member of the audience, in search of dramatic satisfaction, interrupts the performance. Despite everyone's energetic efforts, Victor, like Didi and Gogo in *Godot*, does not move.

Should *Eleutheria* be fully staged, it would need an expert cast of comical tragedians and a director with the imagination of Beckett himself, or an Ingmar Bergman with a surrealistic sense of humour. It would also benefit from judicious editing in the first and third acts (one can anticipate an objection from the Beckett estate) and the smoothing over of awkward passages in Mr. Brodsky's translation. The play, a valuable addition to Beckett's body of work, will be of interest to anyone concerned with the author's art and with exploratory theatre. De-jettisoned, *Eleutheria* has found its freedom.

Afterword

Once on a trip to Provence, I visited Roussillon, where Beckett had been in hiding during World War II. Expecting a quiet bourgeois community, I was surprised to see a picturesque hilltop town. On the long winding road leading to the centre, artists at easels were painting the scenery. Walking through the town past the tourists, one could find no mark of Beckett, no feeling that this had ever been his home. But it was here that he spent several crucial years, writing *Watt* and gathering impressions for what turned out to be *Waiting for Godot*. Apparently, wherever Beckett went, he carried his world and his solitude with him.

For the last three decades of his life, he lived in a modern, undistinguished building on Boulevard St. Jacques in the 14th arrondissement of Paris. His home, in common with so much else in his life, was kept private. Many of his friends never visited him there, but met him, as I generally did, in his favourite café in the PLM hotel down the street. The hotel has since become one of the Sofitel chain. The section is working-class, and Beckett was its most celebrated resident.

After Beckett's death in 1989, Edward Beckett had his uncle's apartment painted and refurbished, and he and his family stay there whenever they are in Paris. Several original items remain, including the piano played by Samuel Beckett and his wife Suzanne, and the writer's study is virtually intact. Edward Beckett is adamant about not opening the home as a museum.

On a rainy afternoon in February of 1996, I visited Beckett's apartment for the first time. My guide was Yves

Colleau, an elderly downstairs neighbour, who brought along his-son-in law as interpreter. Though certainly not gregarious, the Becketts were friendly with a few of their neighbours, including Colleau, and Suzanne had given piano lessons to the daughter of the family next door. Because Beckett was besieged by uninvited visitors, Colleau had 'a special knock' so that he would know it was not a stranger trying to intrude. Put together from an apartment and an adjoining studio, Beckett's home has five small rooms. It is exceedingly modest considering the author's great literary success. He lived completely without ostentation and without a hint of luxury.

In his study, everything is precisely in order. An office-style metal desk faces a Cubist painting by Geer van Velde. Beckett often changed the art (from a Geer van Velde to a Bram van Velde to Henri Hayden) but always had a painting in that space. There are no other pictures on the grey green walls. Behind the desk is a small, worn, rust-coloured leather chair, which Suzanne had found at a Parisian market. It is short, almost child-size. Sitting in the chair, I found it difficult to believe that Beckett, with his long legs, could have been comfortable. But at this desk – and in his country home in Ussy – he worked and answered his deluge of mail. On the desk is a tray (in which he kept stationery and a paper knife for opening letters) and next to it is his telephone, with no number on it. There is an extension of the desk for a typewriter, now occupied by Edward Beckett's computer; on the floor are a portable typewriter and a small electric radiator. On a cold day such as this one, Beckett would wear a heavy sweater while he worked.

Along with the desk and chair, the most notable feature in the study is a bookcase, which wraps around the rear and side wall, and is filled, floor to ceiling, with Beckett's books. A circular stepladder allows one to reach the upper shelves. That ladder replaces a small three-step aluminium ladder that Beckett had used. The books are carefully alphabetised from Arrabal to Yeats, and include Jane Austen (*Selected Letters* and *Northanger Abbey*), Baudelaire, Dante, Dostoyevsky, Samuel Johnson, Pepys, Schopenhauer, Simplicissimus's *Grimmelshausen* and Voltaire. There are two shelves devoted to Joyce and one shelf to Yeats.

In addition to Arrabal and Pinter, both of whom inscribed their works to Beckett (Arrabal with 'admiration' and 'tendresse'), there are plays by Chekhov, Strindberg, Pinget and Wilde. Nancy Cunard and Thomas McGreevy each signed copies of their books, in McGreevy's case a study of T.S. Eliot. Alexander Schneider inscribed his memoir *A Musician's Life*. Nearby is Ernest Jones's life of Freud. Beckett also had a small collection of books about artists: Goya, Max Ernst, Picasso and Avigdor Arikha, who was a friend of his. Easily reachable from the desk are dictionaries and encyclopaedias in English and French, books on language, a *Roget's Thesaurus*, the *Oxford Companion to Music*. These books in particular look well used; several have lost their covers. On a high shelf are *Portrait of Irish Medicine* and a large bound doctoral thesis on Beckett written by a Stanford University student he met in Paris in 1982.

Beckett was surrounded by his own complete works, in various editions, from paperback to leatherbound, in English, French, German and Japanese, and by – one surprise – a row of books about him and his writing, critical studies by S.E. Gontarski and James Knowlson, among others. Deirdre Bair's biography is noticeably absent.

On a low shelf are chess books by Arrabal and Bobby Fischer (*My 60 Memorable Games*), among others, and several pocket-size chessboards. Next to them are maps, including a London A to Z streetguide and a Companion Guide to *The Country Round Paris*, a sign that Beckett was not sedentary. Nearby are a clock, binoculars and a gnarled corkscrew.

Heavy shutters shield the room's single window. Perched on the sill is a metal figure created by the Russian sculptor, Sidur. It is entitled *Invalide*, and in all seasons it remains exposed to the weather of the world. Though one might tend

187

to draw a parallel between the sculpture and its stoical owner, I could sense Beckett's reproof: no symbols where none intended. Especially on this overcast day, the view was exceedingly bleak. To the north one could see the Santé prison, a large, drab, armoury-like building with many windows (each represents a cell, from which inmates wave to the outside world). To the left of the prison are a hospital and a weather station.

As I looked out of Beckett's window, I thought of homes of other writers: the warmth and intimacy of Balzac's library; Edith Wharton sitting up in bed while she wrote; Herman Melville at work in Massachusetts, facing a rolling hill, humpbacked like a whale. Beckett's room – and his view – is, of course, Beckettian. At his desk, without distraction, he could explore his own interior vision. One could imagine him sitting here, composing *A Piece of Monologue*, *Rockaby* and other dead-of-night soliloquies and, in his last year, *What is the Word*, his final expression of the 'folly' of trying to use language to account for life. As promised, the study was filled with echoes and emanations of Beckett.

Acknowledgments

I want to thank all the people who have spoken to me over the years about their relationship with Samuel Beckett and with his work. Some but not all of them are represented in this book. They include: Edward Albee, Fernando Arrabal, Deirdre Bair, Edward Beckett, Linda Ben-Zvi, Tom and Helen Gary Bishop, John Calder, Ruby Cohn, Hume Cronyn, Martha Fehsenfeld, Athol Fugard, Martin Garbus, S. E. Gontarski, Dustin Hoffman, Israel Horovitz, Bill Irwin, James Knowlson, Bert Lahr, Jack MacGowran, Gregory Mosher, Mike Nichols, Harold Pinter, Barney Rosset, Alan Schneider, Martin Segal, Tom Stoppard, Jessica Tandy, Deborah Warner, David Warrilow, Billie Whitelaw and Irene Worth. My thanks also to Nick Hern, who edited and published this book as well as its predecessors, *Conversations with Pinter* and *Conversations with Stoppard*; my agent Owen Laster; my wife Ann for her infallible editing and her continuing encouragement, and our son Ethan for moving me closer to the cutting edge of technology. My appreciation also to Carol Coburn at the Times in New York and Pamela Kent at the Times in London. Most of all, I want to thank Samuel Beckett.

The obituary and selected reviews and essays were printed in the New York Times.* Some of the material in the introduction and in other sections of the book appeared in different form in the New York Times. A limited part of the conversation with Bert Lahr appeared in Newsweek. Extracts from Beckett's letters are reproduced by permission of the Samuel Beckett Estate.

*Copyright 1969, 70, 76, 77, 80, 81, 83, 86, 89, 90, 92, 93, 95 by The New York Times Company. Reprinted by permission.

Index